The Collected Poems of
Oscar Wilde

The Collected Poems of
Oscar Wilde

*With an Introduction and Notes
by Dr Anne Varty*

Wordsworth Poetry Library

This edition published 1994 by Wordsworth Editions Ltd,
Cumberland House, Crib Street, Ware, Hertfordshire SG12 9ET

2 4 6 8 10 9 7 5 3 1

ISBN 1 85326 453 9

Typeset by Antony Gray
Printed and bound in Great Britain by
Mackays of Chatham plc, Chatham, Kent

INTRODUCTION

The Ballad of Reading Gaol (1898) is the masterpiece of Wilde's poetic achievement and his most famous poem, the last work he completed between his release from prison in May 1897 and his death in November 1900. It was first published anonymously, signed only 'C.3.3.', the number of the cell in Reading Gaol where Wilde was kept in solitary confinement for two years. It is printed here alongside his first collection of verse, *Poems* (1881), with which as a young man of twenty-seven Wilde announced his arrival on London's literary scene and made his ambitions known. These bookends of Wilde's career as a writer, *Poems* and *The Ballad of Reading Gaol*, were first placed in a single collection of poems in 1908 by Wilde's friend and literary executor, Robert Ross. From 1905 Ross worked hard as an editor of Wilde's writings in order to rehabilitate the reputation of his dead friend and to bring Wilde's estate, bankrupt in 1895, back into credit for the benefit of Wilde's sons, Cyril and Vyvyan. Ross felt responsible for this enterprise not just as Wilde's appointed executor but also because he himself was Wilde's first male lover and so could be seen to have set Wilde on the path which led to his humiliation and imprisonment for the practice of homosexuality. The volume of poetry you hold in your hand is a direct result of Ross's editorial enterprise, because the selection and arrangement of texts is the same as that which he published as Wilde's *Poems* in 1909, the second and slightly altered edition of the 1908 collection.

Ross opened the volume with Wilde's 1881 collection *Poems*, after which he placed a selection of Wilde's 'Uncollected Poems'. These had been published previously in various magazines and journals, except for 'Désespoir' and 'Pan' which Ross discovered in manuscript amongst Wilde's papers and published for the first time in 1908. Following this section he placed the long erotic poem *The Sphinx* (1894), which had first appeared in an exquisitely bound volume, embossed in white and gold, with suitably erotic illustrations by the decadent designer Charles Ricketts. Next came *The Ballad of Reading Gaol* (1898). He closed the volume with a poem from Wilde's student days at Oxford, *Ravenna* (1878), the title of the Oxford University competition which Wilde entered, fortuitously having visited Ravenna, the city of Dante and Byron, in 1877. With this poem he won the prestigious Newdigate Prize for Poetry, and like John Ruskin who won the prize in 1839 and Matthew Arnold in 1843, he read his winning poem aloud to an audience of academics in the Sheldonian Theatre in Oxford in 1878.

Life and Work

Apart from *The Ballad of Reading Gaol* Wilde is rarely remembered as a poet. This aspect of his work has been eclipsed both by his extraordinary life story and by his glittering success with the society comedies, *Lady Windermere's Fan* (1892), *A Woman of No Importance* (1893), *The Importance of Being Earnest* (1895) and *An Ideal Husband* (1895). His popular reputation as a writer depends on these plays, and on the novel *The Picture of Dorian Gray* (1890). Wilde arrived at these successes by a fairly conventional route, but his departure from them was abrupt, unique and tragic. Born in Dublin in 1854, he studied Greek and Latin first at Trinity College, Dublin, and then, from 1873, at Magdalen College, Oxford. On graduating he moved to London where he set about establishing himself as a writer. The publication of *Poems*, at his own expense in 1881, was his opening move in this campaign which had so far been sustained by his flamboyant personality. *Poems* proved a highly effective piece of self-advertisement, clinching his reputation as a member of the fashionable artistic élite. Although most reviews were far from favourable, the rewards of notoriety were immediate. In 1882 he was sponsored by the theatre producer D'Oyly Carte to lecture across North America. Wilde's appearances were to act as promotion for the American tour of D'Oyly Carte's production of the Gilbert and Sullivan opera *Patience*, which was held to portray a satirised version of Wilde himself in the character of Bunthorne, an effete poet of the Aesthetic Movement.

For Wilde, all publicity was good publicity. Having taken America by storm he returned to London in 1883 where he spent most of the decade working as a journalist, writing book reviews and magazine fiction, and editing *The Lady's World*, which he renamed *The Woman's World*, from 1887 to 1889. His departures from London during this period included an extended visit to Paris for three months in the early spring of 1883. In 1884 Wilde celebrated his marriage to Constance Lloyd with a honeymoon in Paris. His family life was quickly established with the birth of their sons Cyril in 1885 and Vyvyan in 1886. These respectable versions of his personal and his professional lives coincided, however, with his cultivation of an outlawed and adulterous life through the practice of homosexuality from 1886 onwards. The theme of leading a double life, outwardly beautiful and inwardly corrupt, was the subject of his first big literary success, the controversial novel *The Picture of Dorian Gray*, published in 1890.

Successes on the London stage followed soon. *The Importance of Being Earnest* opened to huge critical acclaim on Valentine's Day in 1895. Two weeks later Wilde found a card left for him at the Albemarle Club by the Marquess of Queensberry which read 'For Oscar Wilde posing as a somdomite'. Wilde had been conducting a passionate and dangerously public affair with Lord Alfred Douglas, nicknamed 'Bosie', the youngest son of the Marquess of Queensberry, since they first met in 1891. The accusation on the card was misspelled but still undeniable, yet Wilde took the Marquess of Queensberry to court for libel. Wilde lost the case, and was immediately charged by the Crown for offences under the 1885 Criminal Law Amendment Act which criminalised all homosexual activity, irrespective of the age or consent of the parties involved. The first jury was unable to reach a verdict and a second trial was called. In May 1895, Wilde received the most severe punishment which the law imposed for this crime, two years' imprisonment with hard labour. Wilde was released from Reading Gaol in 1897, publicly humiliated and inwardly broken. He spent the last three years of his life in exile in Europe, often using the pseudonym 'Sebastian Melmoth'. Wilde composed this name after the Christian martyr St Sebastian, mentioned in the poem 'The Grave of Keats' (p. 71), and the eponymous hero of *Melmoth the Wanderer* (1820), a novel by Charles Maturin who was an ancestor of Wilde in his mother's family. He died in Paris on 30 November 1900. In 1909 Wilde's remains were moved from the cemetery at Bagneux to Père Lachaise where Jacob Epstein's monument of the winged sphinx was placed to mark his grave. Lines from *The Ballad of Reading Gaol* are cut into the stone:

> And alien tears will fill for him
> Pity's long-broken urn,
> For his mourners will be outcast men,
> And outcasts always mourn.   (p. 151)

Poetic Reputation and Reception

As different features of Wilde's extraordinary life have captured the public imagination at various times, so different poems have been the subject of various kinds of scrutiny. For example, in 1882, in America, the press particularly admired the young Irishman's anti-imperialist poem 'Ave Imperatrix' ('Hail, Empress', p. 2), which ends by expressing a hope that a 'young Republic' can emerge from the bloodied 'crimson seas of war' (p. 5) that mark Britain's imperialist endeavours of the nineteenth century. In 1895, at the time of Wilde's trials, when there was consternation at the apparent iniquity of such a dazzling society star, a pamphlet called *The Life of Oscar Wilde as Prosecutor and Prisoner* called attention to the elegy 'Requiescat' ('May She Rest', p. 18). This was a poem which Wilde had written in 1874 in memory of his sister Isola who died in 1867 shortly before her tenth birthday, when Wilde was twelve.

> Tread lightly, she is near
>   Under the snow,
> Speak gently, she can hear
>   The daisies grow.   (p. 18)

The pamphlet describes this as the 'choicest specimen' of his poetry, and points implicitly to the gulf that separates this hushed expression of grief for lost innocence and beauty from the trumpeted public perception of the criminalised Wilde. This was also the only poem by Wilde which Yeats chose to anthologise in his 1895 edition of *A Book of Irish Verse*.

The evidence that Wilde's first collection of verse was well received by readers is not matched by the reviews which *Poems* received on its first appearance in 1881, when it met with hostility. Reviewers objected in particular to what they perceived as the derivative nature of the collection. The satirical magazine *Punch* published a parodic portrait of Wilde's face in the centre of a sunflower, with the caption:

> Aesthete of Aesthetes!
> What's in a name?
> The poet is WILDE,
> But his poetry's tame.   (*Punch*, 25 June 1881)

With ludicrous arrogance, members of the Oxford University Student Union even returned their gift of a copy on the grounds that the contents were plagiarised:

It is not that these poems are thin – and they *are* thin: it is not that they are immoral – and they *are* immoral . . . it is that they are for the most part not by their putative father at all, but by a number of better known and more deservedly reputed authors . . . The Union Library already contains better and fuller editions of all these poets.[1]

It is true that throughout the 1881 collection Wilde can be seen sorting through a wardrobe of different poetic styles, trying on one after another to see what suits him best and always wearing his erudition on his sleeve. He tries on the Pre-Raphaelite ballad ('Ballade de Marguerite', p. 73), the moral sententiousness of Matthew Arnold ('Humanitad', p. 96) and Swinburne's erotic religiosity ('La Bella Donna Della Mia Mente', p. 47); he presents nature through Keats's cloying enchantment ('Charmides', p. 49) or Coleridge's pantheism ('Panthea', p. 83). But Wilde never deploys another writer's style without a deliberate acknowledgement that this is what he is doing, managing simultaneously to nod a compliment and to assert his rivalry. Early experimentation with different conventions also makes Wilde's verse typical of an era, and it can be read to give insight to a century of poetic practice.

Readers and reviewers were also divided about the achievement of *The Ballad of Reading Gaol*. It sold over seven thousand copies within sixteen months of its first publication in February 1898, and has remained internationally popular ever since. But early reviewers did not share this enthusiasm. The anonymous review in the *Athenaeum* stated that it was 'authentic: hence its worth', but continued, 'the poem is not great, is not entirely trustworthy; but in so far as it is the faithful record of experiences through which the writer – C.3.3. – has passed, it is good literature' (28 February 1898). More pointed criticism came from W. E. Henley in *Outlook* (5 March 1898) who judged:

In matter, it is a patchwork of what is and what is not. Here it is instinct and vigorous with veracity; there it is flushed and stertorous with sentimentalism. It is carefully written and elaborately designed; yet it is full fifty stanzas too long . . .

Wilde's uncollected poems have received little critical attention, in part because their initial publication in disparate journals made them inaccessible as a body of work. Recent interest in his impressionist lyrics which are included in the 'Uncollected Poems' section of this volume is signalled by the fact that in 1987 the editor of *The New Oxford Book of Victorian Verse*,

---

1 Oliver Elton, cited in Richard Ellmann, *Oscar Wilde*, Hamish Hamilton, London 1987, p. 140

Christopher Ricks, chose to represent Wilde's work with 'Les Ballons' (p. 119) and 'Symphony in Yellow' (p. 121), as well as *The Ballad of Reading Gaol*. In making this selection Ricks presents a sample of Wilde's most impressive shorter poetry which foreshadows the poetic imagism of the twentieth century.

Aesthetic Poetry

Some of Wilde's most striking poems are those in which he puts the doctrines of aestheticism into practice, where he sheds the mannered archaisms in diction, the insistent references to classical mythology and the echoing of other poets. Instead he allows both his range of reference and his style of perception to become thoroughly modern and thoroughly his own. He draws inspiration from the doctrines of his Oxford mentor Walter Pater and from the practice of French Impressionist painters. Wilde came to know Pater's influential collection of essays *Studies in the History of the Renaissance* (1873) as a student at Oxford. In the 'Conclusion' to this volume Pater asserted that life was in constant flux, subjecting the individual to a potentially overwhelming whirlpool of transient experience:

> Experience seems to bury us under a flood of external objects . . . But when reflexion begins to play upon those objects they are dissipated under its influence . . . each object is loosed into a group of impressions – colour, odour, texture – in the mind of the observer.[2]

The only way to pull free of this experiential whirlpool, to find a stable permanence within the flux, was through art. For Pater and his followers, including Wilde, only the organising power of art could arrest the rush of time and yield a heightened consciousness to give insight to experience. Pater declared that art would allow the individual's awareness 'to burn always with this hard, gem-like flame, to maintain this ecstasy' (*Renaissance*, 189). This statement is the principal formulation underlying the Aesthetic Movement and the practice of 'art for art's sake' in Britain.

Pater's influence on Wilde's poetry is particularly evident in the impressionist poems such as 'Impression du Matin' (1881, p. 41), 'Les Silhouettes' (1881, p. 70), 'Impression. Le Réveillon'(1881, p. 89), 'Les Ballons' (1887, p. 119), or 'Symphony in Yellow' (1889, p. 121). Wilde captures shifting arrangements of colour and movement in stanzas such as:

---

2 Walter Pater, *The Renaissance. Studies in Art and Poetry*, ed. Donald L. Hill (1873; University of California Press, Berkeley, Los Angeles and London 1980), p. 187. Hereafter referred to as *Renaissance*.

> Big barges full of yellow hay
> Are moved against the shadowy wharf,
> And, like a yellow silken scarf,
> The thick fog hangs along the quay.
>
> ('Symphony in Yellow', p. 121)

or

> Against these turbid turquoise skies
> The light and luminous balloons
> Dip and drift like satin moons,
> Drift like silken butterflies.
>
> ('Les Ballons', p. 119)

Here the lyrical voice seizes on a transient moment and lifts it above the ephemeral, fixing and interpreting what is seen, turning sight into vision. So the fog is 'like a yellow silken scarf' and the balloons 'drift like satin moons'. In each case the impression is contained by verbs in the present tense, to indicate both immediacy and stasis. The rhyme scheme of these stanzas, a b b a, compounds the idea that artifice can check flight: the centrally placed rhyming couplet hurries the stanza along, while the last rhyme sends us back to the start and seems to arrest the progress of the subject. The underlying rhythm of iambic tetrameter also works to contain flux as it modulates between swiftly moving polysyllables and more ponderous monosyllables.

In 'Symphony in Yellow', Wilde plays with the paradoxes that are involved in painting, seeing or writing about fog, which after all is normally thought of as something which impedes vision rather than enhances it. Fog supplied him with a metaphor for how the artist can alter the perceptual range of his audience. In *The Decay of Lying* (1891) he asks facetiously:

> Where, if not from the Impressionists, do we get those wonderful brown fogs that come creeping down our streets, blurring the gas-lamps and changing the houses into monstrous shadows? . . . The extraordinary change that has taken place in the climate of London during the last ten years is entirely due to a particular school of Art.[3]

Wilde's impressionism can be seen to anticipate aspects of twentieth-century modernism in work by poets such as Ezra Pound or T. S. Eliot, who wrote in 'The Love Song of J. Alfred Prufrock':

3 Oscar Wilde, *Complete Works* (HarperCollins Publishers, Glasgow 1994), p. 1086. Hereafter referred to as *Works*.

> The yellow fog that rubs its back upon the windowpanes,
> The yellow smoke that rubs its muzzle on the windowpanes
> Licked its tongue into the corners of the evening.

Where Wilde had used a simile to describe the fog ('like a yellow silken scarf'), Eliot uses a metaphor, describing the fog as though it were a cat. Eliot's device is a more extreme example of the aesthetics which Wilde propounded, namely that the artist is omnipotent in creating the reader's frame of reference and manner of seeing.

The title 'Symphony in Yellow' reveals a further strand to Wilde's artistic allegiances since it emphasises the musical quality of the poem. It deliberately recalls the way in which Whistler named his paintings as though they were pieces of music. Whistler's *Nocturne in Blue and Gold: Old Battersea Bridge* (1872/3) is a well-known example of the way in which his titles stake a claim on the inter-relationship of music and painting, and it is a work which gives the first line of Wilde's 'Impression du Matin', 'The Thames nocturne of blue and gold' (p. 41). In choosing such names Whistler draws the attention of the spectator away from the representational aspect of the painting and asks them to consider first the abstract arrangement of colour and form which the canvas presents. For both Wilde and Whistler the control which the artist holds over the perceptions of the reader or spectator is determined by the deployment of artistic form. In 1877, Pater framed a theoretical expression of the primary importance of form, already evident in artistic practice, with his assertion *'all art constantly aspires towards the condition of music'* (*Renaissance*, p. 106). With this he meant to emphasise the abstract and purely sensuous pleasure which a work of art could yield, untroubled by narrative content or representation.

Synaesthesia: Poetry, Music and Painting

Pater's statement of the primacy of music as an artistic model and his insistence that the initial impression made by a work of art is abstract rather than representational reassert the aesthetics of synaesthesia for Wilde and his generation of poets. Synaesthesia had been traditional since the work of the Romantic poets and holds that all the arts are mutually enhancing and metaphorically equivalent in the evocation of sensuous response from their audience. For Wilde, music does not function as just a metaphor for what he hoped to achieve with his poetry, but it is materially significant in the communicative power of his verse. Some of his poems he wrote specifically 'for music', such as 'Endymion' (p. 46) or 'From Spring

Days to Winter' (p. 111), while the titles of other poems such as 'Chanson' ('Song', p. 48) or 'Αἴλινον, αἴλινον . . . ' (Sing the Song of Woe, the Song of Woe, But May the Good Prevail', p. 112) call for musical performance, however inwardly the reader may respond.

Rhythm and rhyme are the two principal musical tools at the poet's disposal. That Wilde viewed them as interdependent and that he found liberation within their formal constraints is evident from his comments in *The Critic as Artist* (1891):

> Rhyme, that exquisite echo which in the Muse's hollow hill creates and answers its own voice; rhyme, which in the hands of the real artist becomes not merely a material element of metrical beauty, but a spiritual element of thought and passion also, waking a new mood, it may be, or stirring a fresh train of ideas, or opening by mere sweetness and suggestion of sound some golden door at which the Imagination itself has knocked in vain; rhyme which can turn man's utterance to the speech of gods; rhyme, the one chord we have added to the Greek lyre . . .
>
> (*Works*, p. 1111)

The pleasure that Wilde took in manipulating these features of verse can be judged from his masterful preference for tight formal structures, such as the sonnet, the villanelle, the sustained stanzaic narrative, and even the ballad.

Wilde couples his foregrounding of the musicality of his verse with a strong sense of its pictorial quality. Wilde's imagination is profoundly visual. As a theatre critic he announced that 'theatrical audiences are far more impressed by what they look at than by what they listen to',[4] and as a poet he both created arresting images and made free use of references to existing works of art. The first of Wilde's impressionist lyrics is 'Impression du Matin' (p. 41) which opens the 'Wind Flowers' section of the 1881 collection. The title of this poem recalls the English title of Claude Monet's painting *Impression: Sunrise*, which was exhibited in Paris in 1874. One art critic, wishing to ridicule the style of Monet and his contemporaries, dubbed this school of painting *impressionisme* and so unwittingly christened this influential movement. Wilde's choice of title therefore signals his aesthetic allegiances. The title of the lyric 'Impression. Le Réveillon' (p. 89) also invites painterly comparison. *Réveillon* is a technical term from French painting, which refers to the dramatic effect of allowing brilliant

---

4 Oscar Wilde, 'Shakespeare on Scenery', *Dramatic Review*, 14 March 1885

light to illuminate a predominantly dark composition. In English the conventional term for this is drawn from Italian, *chiaroscuro*. Wilde's lyric is animated by the observation of various effects of dawning light. The first stanza closes with an image which gives this dawn a metaphorical significance of renaissance or rebirth: 'The dawn is rising from the sea,/ Like a white lady from her bed', recalling Botticelli's *Birth of Venus* and participating in Pater's school of thought that the Aesthetic Movement of the late nineteenth century constituted a rebirth of artistic sensibility. This poem opens the so-called 'Fourth Movement' of the 1881 collection, the last group of shorter poems before the concluding 'Humanitad' and 'Flower of Love'. The title, 'The Fourth Movement', itself asserts a further commitment to synaesthesia, since it is actually the sixth movement within that collection. But Wilde wants his book to establish an association with symphonic form, a musical composition which conventionally ends with a fourth movement, and in so doing he again anticipates the work of modernists such as T. S. Eliot's *Four Quartets*.

Whistler is the artist whose paintings are most frequently invoked in Wilde's poetry. For example the first two stanzas of 'In the Gold Room. A Harmony' (p. 72) invite comparison with three works by Whistler. The first is *The Music Room* (1860), which Whistler later titled *Harmony in Green and Rose*, emphasising the abstract quality of his painting with music as the model. The second is *At the Piano* (1859), and the third, *A Harmony in Yellow and Gold: The Gold Girl* (1876). But this is not the only school of painting to which Wilde refers. The last stanza of 'Impressions 1. Les Silhouettes',

> And overhead the curlews cry,
> Where through the dusky upland grass
> The young brown-throated reapers pass,
> Like silhouettes against the sky.   (p. 70)

brings to life Millet's *The Sower* (1850). Perhaps the most concealed reference to a specific painting occurs in the final stanza of 'My Voice', the closing utterance of a duologue about dying love:

> But all this crowded life has been to thee
> No more than lyre, or lute, or subtle spell
> Of viols, or the music of the sea
> That sleeps, a mimic echo, in the shell.   (p. 94)

Here the lyrical voice constructs his beloved in the image of Leonardo's *Mona Lisa*, as the portrait comes to Wilde refracted through Pater's account of Leonardo's painting. One of the most memorable passages in Pater's *Renaissance* is his description of the *Mona Lisa*, in which he envisions the mysterious figure as an enduring *femme fatale*:

> She is older than the rocks among which she sits; like the vampire, she has been dead many times, and learned the secrets of the grave; and has been a diver in deep seas, and keeps their fallen day about her . . . and all this has been to her but as the sound of lyres and flutes, and lives only in the delicacy with which it has moulded the changing lineaments, and tinged the eyelids and the hands.
>
> (*Works*, p. 1126; *Renaissance*, p. 99)

Wilde was so impressed by this description that he claims in his critical dialogue *The Critic as Artist* (1891) to have learned it by heart, and recited it in front of the painting in the Louvre in an act of aesthetic adoration and worship. 'And so,' Wilde adds, 'the picture becomes more wonderful to us than it really is . . . and the music of the mystical prose is as sweet in our ears as was the flute-player's music that lent to the lips of La Gioconda those subtle and poisonous curves' (*Works*, p. 1126). In the poem 'My Voice', his invocation of these linked works, the painting and the prose description of the *Mona Lisa*, shows him fashioning the lady to whom the lyric is directed according to the late nineteenth-century stereotype of the *femme fatale*.

Just as Wilde's poetry offers rich responses to music and the visual arts, so reciprocally his verse itself has inspired creative work from musicians and graphic artists. In 1911, the composer Jervis-Reade set a number of Wilde's poems to music, following Strauss's 1905 opera score to *Salomé*. Beardsley's illustrations to *Salomé*, Wilde's most poetic play, are well known, and Charles Ricketts's provocative designs for *The Sphinx* were notorious in their day. *The Ballad of Reading Gaol* has a long tradition of illustrations which includes the New York edition of 1907 with drawings by L. J. Wilson, the London edition of 1925 with woodcuts by F. Masereel, lithographs by Z. Gay in 1937 and woodcuts by E. Heckel in 1963 both published in New York, and a German translation published in Amsterdam with illustrations by A. Horodisch-Garman in 1961.

A Manifesto Poem

Wilde launched his 1881 collection *Poems* with an *envoi*, 'Hélas!' ('Alas!'), written to preface the volume. By its position this sonnet carries the authority of a manifesto, and suggests something of the direction Wilde's talents would take. Wilde muses on the seeming conflict between his desire for sensuous indulgence, expressed in terms of Paterian drifting on

the stream of transient experience ('to drift with every passion'), and his
ambition to be a great writer ('I might have trod/The sunlit heights') which
requires the 'austere control' of ascetic withdrawal. The poem comes to
rest on a question, which is an eroticised misquotation from the Bible:

> with a little rod
> I did but touch the honey of romance –
> And must I lose a soul's inheritance?   (p.1)

In I Samuel 14:43 Jonathan, who has broken a sacred fast, tells his father
Saul, 'I did but taste a little honey with the end of the rod that was in mine
hand, and, lo, I must die'. In the Bible, the honey is literally food, but
Wilde turns it into the metaphorical nourishment of 'romance' viewed
with uncanny foresight as the ultimate source of his destruction. However,
Wilde arrived at this metaphor by a scholarly rather than an experiential
route since the reference to Samuel is exactly the one which Pater used in
'Winckelmann', the penultimate essay of *Studies in the History of the
Renaissance*. For Pater, Jonathan's defiance characterises 'the artistic life,
with its inevitable sensuousness' (*Renaissance*, p. 177). Wilde, appropriating
Paterian aesthetics, acknowledges the personal liability that may follow.

'Hélas!' is a poem driven by the kind of paradox that became the hall-
mark of Wilde's style, not least in that it laments the loss of formal aesthetic
control within the tight constraint of the sonnet, exhibiting precisely what
the lyrical voice claims to have lost. It also seems disingenuous to open a
first collection of verse with a rhetorical expression of failure and regret.
Wilde's 'Hélas!', with the introductory description of the poet's soul as 'a
stringed lute on which all winds can play' positions his work in relation to
that of the Romantics. Recalling Coleridge's early conversation poem 'The
Aeolian Harp', Wilde's sonnet bids a nostalgic farewell to the loose
structures of Romantic poetry, asserting instead the primacy of conventional
form that typifies verse of the Aesthetic Movement. Within the 1881
collection Wilde often remembers the work of Romantic poets, only to
lament the passing of their redemptive interpretation of the relationship
between man and nature. For *fin-de-siècle* writers, art intervenes between
man and nature, so music supplies the guiding metaphor for 'Hélas!'. The
poet struggles with 'life's dissonance' to achieve the harmony of art, 'one
clear chord to reach the ears of God', a note of greater significance than 'idle
songs for pipe and virelay'. It is ironic that the 'one clear chord' of Wilde's
poetic achievement, *The Ballad of Reading Gaol*, should indeed fall outside
this first collection, and be heavily indebted to Coleridge's *The Rime of the
Ancient Mariner*. In choosing to give this opening poem a French title Wilde

signals a further departure from British traditions of poetry. He clearly states his espousal of the French *avant garde*, especially the work of Gautier and Baudelaire, which was so influential both for the Aesthetic Movement in Britain as a whole and for his own work in particular.

Poems (1881). A Commentary

Eleutheria

Wilde was only ten years old when his mother, herself a notable poet of the Irish National Movement publishing under the pseudonym 'Speranza', dedicated to him and his elder brother William her collection of revolutionary Irish verse, *Poems* (1864). He never forgot that an important function of poetry, conventional in the nineteenth century, was to express political or moral sentiment. While he returned to this aspect of verse most powerfully in his last work, the first section of his own *Poems* (1881), called 'Eleutheria' (ancient Greek for 'Freedom'), addresses subjects of political concern particular to the late 1870s. These poems display a side of Wilde rarely seen so openly, that of the Victorian reformer rather than the poised dandy. They serve as a useful reminder that Wilde's work in general is informed by an astute sense of the political significance and responsibility of art.

In 'Eleutheria' the sonnet 'To Milton' (p. 7), invoking Wordsworth's 'London, 1802', laments the passing of England as a mighty world power and announces the betrayal of the spirit of democracy by her political leaders. The sonnets 'On the Massacre of the Christians in Bulgaria' (p. 8), 'Quantum Mutata' ('How Much Changed', p. 8)) and 'Libertatis Sacra Fames' ('The Sacred Hunger for Liberty', p. 9) all respond to the Balkan Crisis of 1875–8. During these years the British government under Disraeli refrained from intervention when forces of the Turkish Ottoman Empire suppressed Christian uprisings in Bulgaria and sparked the Russo–Turkish War in 1877. In May 1877 Wilde sent a version of 'On the Massacre of the Christians in Bulgaria' to one of the politicians he most admired, Gladstone, then leader of the Liberal shadow cabinet. Gladstone, in direct opposition to Disraeli, had been campaigning for British intervention in these foreign affairs by circulating pamphlets such as *Bulgarian Horrors and the Question of the East* (1876) and *Lessons in Massacre* (1877). The last sonnet of this section, 'Theoretikos' ('The Thinker', p. 9), signals Wilde's temporary withdrawal from this type of political verse. The poem closes with the statement:

> It mars my calm: wherefore in dreams of Art
> And loftiest culture I would stand apart,
> Neither for God, nor for his enemies.   (p. 9)

This ambition, to concentrate on art rather than politics, is matched by a statement which Wilde made in an interview in America. He was asked why he had left his native Ireland and moved to London: 'I live in London for its artistic life and opportunities . . . There is no lack of culture in Ireland, but it is nearly all absorbed in politics. Had I remained there my career would have been a political one' (*Daily Examiner*, San Francisco, 27 March 1882).

The Garden of Eros

The next section of *Poems* is called 'The Garden of Eros' (1881). This is the first of five long poems which punctuate the groups of shorter verses within the volume and which share stylistic features with the verse of Matthew Arnold and Tennyson. Each of these poems, 'The Garden of Eros', 'The Burden of Itys', 'Charmides', 'Panthea' and 'Humanitad', imitates the metre and verse form of Shakespeare's narrative poem *Venus and Adonis*. Unified by form and style, these poems create a contrapuntal movement in relation to the shorter lyrics of the volume and follow their own sequential arrangement in the order of the seasons. Each seasonal setting reflects the mood of the philosophical narrative. 'The Garden of Eros', a celebratory poem, begins 'It is full summer now', while the last, 'Humanitad', concerning failures and discontents, begins 'It is full winter now'.

'The Garden of Eros' exhibits features which are typical of this first collection of poetry. It is steeped in classical imagery drawn from the world of literature which Wilde had come to know intimately through his study of ancient Greek and Latin. Set against the invocation of the idyllic pastoral values of the ancient world is a picture of destructive nineteenth-century industrialisation. For Wilde, the commercial values of his own century starve the imagination, 'spite of all/Its new-found creeds so sceptical and so dogmatical' (p. 12). Echoing the sentiments of the Victorian sage Thomas Carlyle, who prized the mystically 'invisible' world rather than the mundanely 'visible', Wilde's lyric asks, 'Shall I, the last Endymion, lose all hope/ Because rude eyes peer at my mistress through a telescope!' (p. 15). Rejection of utilitarianism was a powerful motivating force for the poets and writers of the Aesthetic Movement who celebrated instead a creed of 'art for art's sake' to nourish spiritual hunger and feed the imagination with images of beauty. In 'The Garden of Eros' Wilde looks for support for his view of the cultural value of art from other nineteenth-century writers. The refrain of the poem, 'Spirit of Beauty! tarry still awhile' (p. 12), invokes the work of the Romantic poet Shelley and is a partial quotation from his 'Hymn to Intellectual Beauty'. Wilde later had this phrase inscribed on the library wall in his Chelsea home. Within 'The

Garden of Eros' Wilde also admires the work of other Romantics, Keats and Byron, before turning to his contemporaries, the pre-Raphaelites William Morris and Dante Gabriel Rossetti.

Charmides

Amongst these longer works 'Charmides' (1881) was the most notorious, as well as being the poem which Wilde claimed was his 'most finished and perfect' (*Daily Examiner*, 27 March 1882). The story of 'Charmides' is about perverse erotic desire and it has a classical source, in Lucian's *Essays in Portraiture*. Wilde's version tells of a beautiful boy who falls in love with the goddess Athena. He breaks into her temple and makes love to her statue,

> Undid the cuirass, and the crocus gown
> And bared the breasts of polished ivory,
> Till from the waist the peplos falling down
> Left visible the secret mystery . . .   (p. 52)

As punishment the goddess ensures that he is drowned. A nymph finds 'the boy's pale body stretched upon the sand' (p. 59) and falls in love with it, only to die for 'raptures unenjoyed' and 'all the pain of things unsatisfied' (p. 65). Finally the goddess of love, Venus, takes pity on the pair and revives them in the Underworld where 'all his hoarded sweets were hers to kiss,/And all her maidenhood was his to slay' (p. 69). Even Wilde's friend and most favourable reviewer, Oscar Browning, was hard pressed to find something good to say about this poem. 'Charmides' had 'music, beauty, imagination and power; but the story, as far as there is one, is most repulsive. Mr Wilde has no magic to veil the hideousness of a sensuality which feeds on statues and dead bodies' (*Academy*, 30 July 1881). The difficulties which Wilde brought upon himself with this poem did not end with the reviewers. Wilde's biographer Richard Ellmann describes how Canon Miles, the father of Wilde's London housemate Frank Miles, was so outraged by 'Charmides' that he forced an incensed Oscar to find somewhere else to live.[5]

Rosa Mystica

Where Wilde breaks free from the influence of his forebears and contemporaries is in the use of conventional verse forms to mask autobiographical ambitions or concerns. While this is most conspicuous in

5 Ellmann, op. cit., p. 142

his use of the ballad to tell his own painful prison story, it is a technique already apparent in his earlier verse. For example, the drama of his uncertainty about orthodox Christian faith and his dilemma about whether to convert to Roman Catholicism, which he experienced on his Easter journey through Italy and Greece in 1877, are played out in the 'Rosa Mystica' section of *Poems*. The sonnet 'Easter Day' (p. 24), in which Wilde describes the Easter procession of Pope Pius IX, with whom he had had a personal audience during his visit to Rome, captures this. The lyrical voice is first enthralled by the magnificent display, 'in splendour and in light the Pope passed home', but then rejects these earthly trappings of religious power. 'My heart stole back across the wide wastes of years/ To one who wandered by a lonely sea/ and sought in vain for any place of rest.' The poem comes to rest on an image of Christ as an outcast with which the lyrical voice identifies. This anticipates Wilde's construction of himself in his prison autobiography *De Profundis*, and in *The Ballad of Reading Gaol*: 'I, only I, must wander wearily,/ And bruise my feet, and drink wine salt with tears'. The drama of Wilde's crisis of faith ends with victory for the spirit of Hellenism, signalled by the poem which closes this section, 'The New Helen' (p. 26), a grandiose celebration of the famous society beauty Lillie Langtry ('Lily of love, pure and inviolate!') who became the not so inviolate mistress of the Prince of Wales.

Impressions de Théâtre

In the last year of his life Wilde declared that the three women he had most admired were Queen Victoria, Sarah Bernhardt and Lillie Langtry, and that he would gladly have married any one of them. The mature writer can laugh at the pretensions of his youth, while as a young man Wilde used his art to court a number of leading society figures as part of his strategy of self-aggrandisement during the late 1870s. The section 'Impressions de Théâtre' is a good example, in which he admires three major theatre stars of the late nineteenth century, Henry Irving, Sarah Bernhardt and Ellen Terry, all of whom became his friends. In the light of his own subsequent success as a dramatist Wilde's satirical scrutiny of the contemporary stage reveals a young playwright in the wings. The sonnet 'Fabien dei Franchi' is about Henry Irving's role in Boucicault's *The Corsican Brothers*. In the octet Wilde mocks the tricks and clichés of spine-chilling melodrama,

> The silent room, the heavy creeping shade,
>   The dead that travel fast, the opening door,
>   The murdered brother rising through the floor.   (p. 80)

Later, Wilde would deploy aspects of the melodramatic imagination in *The Ballad of Reading Gaol*, but here the sonnet turns on the last line of the octet, in which Wilde dismisses these conventional features. 'These things are well enough, – but thou wert made/ For more august creation! frenzied Lear . . . '. Only Shakespeare, Wilde asserts, can supply Irving with roles to match his talent, 'Thou trumpet set for Shakespeare's lips to blow!' Ellen Terry, the subject of three of these five theatre sonnets, is also most properly served by Shakespeare. In 'Camma' (p. 82), the name of the character she played in Tennyson's *The Cup*, Wilde wryly echoes Tennyson's 'The Lady of Shallot' in the penultimate line, 'I am grown sick of unreal passions', before asking Terry to transform the unreal to the real by stepping off stage into a life quickened by theatrical poetry, 'make/ The world thine Actium, me thine Anthony!'

Wilde as Self-Plagiarist

Early reviewers of Wilde's poetry may have been swift to note his debts to other poets, but Wilde was far too self-regarding as a writer to be held up long by the work of others. One of the characteristic features of his work is his habit of plagiarising not others but himself. Just as swathes of dialogue from *The Picture of Dorian Gray* recur in *A Woman of No Importance*, so too his poetry acts as a repository for ideas and images which he would use again elsewhere. For example, the drama of the 1881 poem 'La Fuite de la Lune' ('The Flight of the Moon', p. 70) is re-enacted in his symbolist play *Salomé* (1892) in which the moon may be seen as the most important character. The last stanza of 'La Fuite de la Lune' reads:

> And suddenly the moon withdraws
> Her sickle from the lightening skies,
> And to her sombre cavern flies,
> Wrapped in a veil of yellow gauze.

At the beginning of *Salomé* the Young Syrian notices the appearance of the moon, beginning to establish a symbolic link between Salomé and the moon: 'She is like a little princess who wears a yellow veil' (*Works*, p. 583). At the end of the play Wilde explores the dramatic effects of what can be achieved when 'suddenly the moon withdraws'. Herod commands, 'Put out the torches! Hide the moon! Hide the stars!' and the stage directions follow: '*The slaves put out the torches. The stars disappear. The great black cloud crosses the moon and conceals it completely*' (*Works*, p. 605). Another, simpler, example of a poem containing the seeds of a more extended piece can be seen in 'Le Jardin de Tuileries' (1885, p. 116). In this poem the lyrical voice describes a winter scene of children at play in the Tuileries park in Paris. The final stanza imagines how a 'black and leafless tree' would respond:

> Ah! cruel tree! If I were you,
> And children climbed me, for their sake
> Though it be winter I would break
> Into spring blossoms white and blue!

This anticipates the magical transformation scene in Wilde's fairy story 'The Selfish Giant' (1888). The giant is so selfish that in his garden it is always winter. But when the children break into his garden to play 'the trees were so glad to have the children back again that they had covered themselves with blossoms, and were waving their arms gently above the children's heads' (*Works*, p. 284).

The Sphinx

In its literary excesses and monstrous couplings, 'Charmides' (1881) anticipates *The Sphinx* (1894), a fairy tale for adults in Wilde's most jewelled and extravagant style. The dynamics of this later poem make it altogether more sinister than 'Charmides' as an exploration of forbidden sexuality. The distancing conventions of antique pastoral are supplanted by the contemporary and intimate night-time setting of the speaker's student bedroom, while a sense of the exotic is maintained not only by the fantastic flights of imagination but also by the unusual formal qualities of the poem. It is arranged in couplets, each line containing sixteen syllables and an internal rhyme. Wilde began to compose this poem in quatrains which used his favoured a b b a rhyme scheme, and then stretched them out to form couplets so that the first rhyming word is placed in the middle of the first line and meets its match in the last word of the couplet. It is a rhyme scheme that creates both dissonance and surprising harmonies, discomforting the reader by making alien territory seem familiar.

  The Sphinx is a monologue addressed to the statue of a sphinx which 'for longer than my fancy thinks . . . has watched me through the shifting gloom' (p. 127). The lyrical voice brings the statue to life: 'Come forth, my lovely seneschal! so somnolent, so statuesque!/Come forth you exquisite grotesque! half woman and half animal!' (p. 127). The speaker questions the sphinx about her memories, first focusing voyeuristically on erotic encounters she has witnessed:

Sing to me of that odorous green eve when crouching
                                                    by the marge
You heard from Adrian's gilded barge the laughter of Antinous

And lapped the stream and fed your drouth and watched
                                        with hot and hungry stare
The ivory body of that rare young slave with his
                                            pomegranate mouth!
                                                    (p. 128)

Interest in such mythically intense encounters is quickly abandoned as the speaker demands closer knowledge of the sphinx herself:

Who were your lovers? Who were they who wrestled for
                                        you in the dust?
Which was the vessel of your Lust? What Leman had you,
                                            every day?
                                                    (p. 129)

The answer conjures an erotic parade of exotic grotesques. The speaker is captivated by the autoeroticism of his voice until, belatedly, he is disgusted by his own excess:

Get hence, you loathsome mystery! Hideous animal, get hence!
You wake in me each bestial sense, you make me what
                                                I would not be.
                                                    (p. 135)

The dismissal and the protestation come too late to carry conviction. The fantasies ostensibly provoked by the sphinx had been contrived by the indulgent imagination of the speaker. Even his protective invocation of the 'one God' ('only one God has let His side be wounded by a soldier's spear', p. 133) fuses a sado-masochistc connotation of Christ on the cross with the homoerotically charged image of the martyr St Sebastian.

The Ballad of Reading Gaol

The Ballad of Reading Gaol comes directly from Wilde's prison experience and adapts the traditional story-telling function of the ballad to fit a contemporary theme. It is dedicated to the memory of 'C. T. W.', Charles Taylor Wooldridge, who was hanged for murdering his wife during the time when Wilde was in Reading Gaol. The ballad is composed of two distinct sections. The first tells the story of how the other prisoners respond to the fact that one of their number is condemned to death. The second section, which begins at Part V, develops a polemical discussion about the nature of justice and is a severe indictment of the cruelties of the prison system which picks up a campaign in which Wilde participated following his release. He published two letters in the *Daily Chronicle* to argue for the more humane treatment of prisoners, particularly children: 'The Case of Warder Martin: Some Cruelties of Prison Life' (28 May 1897) and 'Prison Reform' (24 March 1898).

The two sections of the ballad, the narrative and the discursive moralising about justice, are linked by the Christian sense of brotherhood. In the first section of the poem the narrator establishes a moral likeness between the condemned man, himself, the other prisoners and the reader by the use of the refrain, 'Yet each man kills the thing he loves,/ By each let this be heard' (p. 137). It insists on a tragic double bind of the human condition, which demands compassion rather than condemnation. In the closing section this insight is developed into argument in which the narrative voice asserts that since nobody is innocent, nobody has the right to impose punishment and the ultimate dispensation of justice rests with God. Wilde adapted this resonant phrase from the trial scene of Shakespeare's *Merchant of Venice*, in which Bassanio asks Shylock, 'Do all men kill the things they do not love?' (4, 1, 66). The scene in Shakespeare's play, which Wilde had mentioned previously in his 1880 sonnet to Ellen Terry, 'Portia'(p. 81), is appropriately echoed in *The Ballad of Reading Gaol* because both works address the subject of justice. Wilde's grim distortion and inversion of Shakespeare's question is equally apt, since the play offers a resolution to the problematic dispensation of justice while Wilde's ballad withholds it. Yet the crux of both *The Merchant of Venice* and *The Ballad of Reading Gaol* is a meditation on the nature of Christian mercy and its relation to crime and punishment.

Wilde's use of the refrain in the ballad creates a unifying effect. It makes the poem itself a cohesive, unified incantation, and it also, thematically, draws the reader in. The ballad deploys other methods to make the reader complicit with the paradox of simultaneously experienced social guilt and spiritual innocence. For example, when the speaker hears a whisper telling him '*That fellow's got to swing*' (p. 136), the immediate response of the poem is for the speaker to internalise and anticipate the experience of hanging:

> Dear Christ! The very prison wall
> Suddenly seemed to reel,

> And the sky above my head became
>> Like a casque of scorching steel;
> And, though I was a soul in pain,
>> My pain I could not feel.   (p. 137)

The statement that the speaker is 'a soul in pain' is one of the first references to Coleridge's ballad *The Rime of the Ancient Mariner* (1798) which is an important precursor to Wilde's. The Ancient Mariner, like Wilde's narrator, is both condemned to tell his story and purified by the act of narration. Both speakers bring messages of salvation to their listeners, while presenting visions of living death, frightening pictures of cruelty and suffering and powerful supernatural forces. Wilde sometimes draws on technical features of Coleridge's ballad to enhance the drama of his own, such as the use of internal rhyme and repetition to create a feverish pace in the stanza that describes the 'crooked shapes of Terror' that haunt the prison:

> With mop and mow, we saw them go,
>> Slim shadows hand in hand:
> About, about, in a ghostly rout
>> They trod a saraband:
> And the damned grotesques made arabesques,
>> Like the wind upon the sand!   (p. 144)

Several contemporary poets also have some influence on *The Ballad of Reading Gaol*, such as Kipling with 'Danny Deever' from *Barrack Room Ballads* (1892) and A. E. Housman with *A Shropshire Lad* (1896), which Housman sent to Wilde on his release.

Many different devices are used to animate this poem, drawn from a variety of poetic traditions. For example, Wilde blends realism about the conditions of prison life with allegory about the fate of the condemned man:

> At six o'clock we cleaned our cells,
>> At seven all was still,
> But the sough and swing of a mighty wing
>> The prison seemed to fill,
> For the Lord of Death with icy breath
>> Had entered in to kill.   (p. 145)

He deploys withering satire to indicate the inadequacy of the prison workers: 'The Doctor said that Death was but/ a scientific fact:/ And twice a day the Chaplain called/ And left a little tract' (p. 141). He uses surrealist vision to suggest how the hanged man will be transfigured by the redeeming Christ, 'Out of his mouth a red, red rose!/Out of his heart a white!' (p. 149), in an image developed directly from the Decadents' idea of regeneration springing from degeneration.

Wilde identifies himself as the narrator with a pun on his name:

> And the wild regrets, and the bloody sweats,
> None knew so well as I:
> For he who lives more lives than one
> More deaths than one must die.   (p. 147)

As these painfully honest lines suggest, the real punishment and grief for his so-called crime are internally experienced and intimately known, not publicly imposed and recognised. In *The Ballad of Reading Gaol* Wilde achieved a great apologia for Christian compassion. He answers the question which he himself had posed eleven years earlier in an article about the social responsibility of poets: 'Who, in the midst of all our poverty and distress, that threatens to become intensified, will step into the breach and rouse us to the almost superhuman effort that is necessary to alter the existing state of things?' (*Pall Mall Gazette*, 17 February 1887).

ANNE VARTY
Royal Holloway

FURTHER READING

K. Beckson (ed.), *Oscar Wilde: The Critical Heritage*, Routledge and Kegan Paul, London 1970 (documents the early reception of Wilde's work with an extensive collection of reviews)

K. Beckson, *An Encyclopaedia of Oscar Wilde*, AMS Press, New York 1998 (offers a wealth of information about Wilde and his work)

R. Ellmann, *Oscar Wilde*, Hamish Hamilton, London 1987 (critical biography)

M. Hicks (ed.), *Selected Poems of Oscar Wilde*, Carcanet, Manchester 1992

C. Nassar, *Into the Demon Universe: A Literary Exploration of Oscar Wilde*, Yale University Press, New Haven 1974 (a general critical study of Wilde, including a chapter on the poetry)

P. Raby (ed.), *The Cambridge Companion to Oscar Wilde*, Cambridge University Press, Cambridge 1997 (a helpful study guide to Wilde, including a chapter on Wilde's poetry)

C. George Sandulescu (ed.), *Rediscovering Oscar Wilde*, Colin Smythe, Gerrards Cross 1994 (published conference papers, which include various scholarly discussions of Wilde's verse)

A. Varty, *A Preface to Oscar Wilde*, Longman, London and New York 1998 (a critical survey of Wilde's work, including a chapter on his poetry)

WEB SITES

http://landow.stg.brown.edu/victorian/victov.html. (This web site offers information about Victorian culture and literature, including poetry and Oscar Wilde.)

CONTENTS

PANTHEA

THE FOURTH MOVEMENT

HUMANITAD

FLOWER OF LOVE

UNCOLLECTED POEMS

THE COLLECTED POEMS
OF OSCAR WILDE

POEMS (1881)

Hélas![1]

To drift with every passion till my soul
Is a stringed lute on which all winds can play,
Is it for this that I have given away
Mine ancient wisdom, and austere control?
Methinks my life is a twice-written scroll
Scrawled over on some boyish holiday
With idle songs for pipe and virelay,
Which do but mar the secret of the whole.
Surely there was a time I might have trod
The sunlit heights, and from life's dissonance
Struck one clear chord to reach the ears of God:
Is that time dead? lo! with a little rod[2]
I did but touch the honey of romance –
And must I lose a soul's inheritance?

ELEUTHERIA[3]

Sonnet to Liberty

Not that I love thy children, whose dull eyes
See nothing save their own unlovely woe,
Whose minds know nothing, nothing care to know, –
But that the roar of thy Democracies,
Thy reigns of Terror, thy great Anarchies,
Mirror my wildest passions like the sea
And give my rage a brother – ! Liberty!
For this sake only do thy dissonant cries
Delight my discreet soul, else might all kings
By bloody knout or treacherous cannonades
Rob nations of their rights inviolate
And I remain unmoved – and yet, and yet,
These Christs that die upon the barricades,
God knows it I am with them, in some things.

Ave Imperatrix[4]

Set in this stormy Northern sea,
    Queen of these restless fields of tide,
England! what shall men say of thee,
    Before whose feet the worlds divide?

The earth, a brittle globe of glass,
    Lies in the hollow of thy hand,
And through its heart of crystal pass,
    Like shadows through a twilight land,

The spears of crimson-suited war,
    The long white-crested waves of fight,
And all the deadly fires which are
    The torches of the lords of Night.

The yellow leopards, strained and lean,
　　The treacherous Russian knows so well,
With gaping blackened jaws are seen
　　Leap through the hail of screaming shell.

The strong sea-lion of England's wars
　　Hath left his sapphire cave of sea
To battle with the storm that mars
　　The stars of England's chivalry.

The brazen-throated clarion blows
　　Across the Pathan's reedy fen,
And the high steeps of Indian snows
　　Shake to the tread of armèd men.

And many an Afghan chief, who lies
　　Beneath his cool pomegranate-trees,
Clutches his sword in fierce surmise
　　When on the mountain-side he sees

The fleet-foot Marri scout, who comes
　　To tell how he hath heard afar
The measured roll of English drums
　　Beat at the gates of Kandahar.

For southern wind and east wind meet
　　Where, girt and crowned by sword and fire,
England with bare and bloody feet
　　Climbs the steep road of wide empire.

O lonely Himalayan height,
　　Grey pillar of the Indian sky,
Where saw'st thou last in clanging flight
　　Our wingèd dogs of Victory?

The almond-groves of Samarcand,
　　Bokhara, where red lilies blow,
And Oxus, by whose yellow sand
　　The grave white-turbaned merchants go:

And on from thence to Ispahan,
    The gilded garden of the sun,
Whence the long dusty caravan
    Brings cedar wood and vermilion;

And that dread city of Cabool
    Set at the mountain's scarpèd feet,
Whose marble tanks are ever full
    With water for the noonday heat:

Where through the narrow straight Bazaar
    A little maid Circassian
Is led, a present from the Czar
    Unto some old and bearded khan, –

Here have our wild war-eagles flown,
    And flapped wide wings in fiery fight;
But the sad dove, that sits alone
    In England – she hath no delight.

In vain the laughing girl will lean
    To greet her love with love-lit eyes:
Down in some treacherous black ravine,
    Clutching his flag, the dead boy lies.

And many a moon and sun will see
    The lingering wistful children wait
To climb upon their father's knee;
    And in each house made desolate

Pale women who have lost their lord
    Will kiss the relics of the slain –
Some tarnished epaulette – some sword –
    Poor toys to soothe such anguished pain.

For not in quiet English fields
    Are these, our brothers, lain to rest,
Where we might deck their broken shields
    With all the flowers the dead love best.

For some are by the Delhi walls,
   And many in the Afghan land,
And many where the Ganges falls
   Through seven mouths of shifting sand.

And some in Russian waters lie,
   And others in the seas which are
The portals to the East, or by
   The wind-swept heights of Trafalgar.

O wandering graves! O restless sleep!
   O silence of the sunless day!
O still ravine! O stormy deep!
   Give up your prey! Give up your prey!

And thou whose wounds are never healed,
   Whose weary race is never won,
O Cromwell's England! must thou yield
   For every inch of ground a son?

Go! crown with thorns thy gold-crowned head,
   Change thy glad song to song of pain;
Wind and wild wave have got thy dead,
   And will not yield them back again.

Wave and wild wind and foreign shore
   Possess the flower of English land –
Lips that thy lips shall kiss no more,
   Hands that shall never clasp thy hand.

What profit now that we have bound
   The whole round world with nets of gold,
If hidden in our heart is found
   The care that groweth never old?

What profit that our galleys ride,
   Pine-forest-like, on every main?
Ruin and wreck are at our side,
   Grim warders of the House of Pain.

Where are the brave, the strong, the fleet?
   Where is our English chivalry?
Wild grasses are their burial-sheet,
   And sobbing waves their threnody.

O loved ones lying far away,
   What word of love can dead lips send!
O wasted dust! O senseless clay!
   Is this the end! is this the end!

Peace, peace! we wrong the noble dead
   To vex their solemn slumber so;
Though childless, and with thorn-crowned head,
   Up the steep road must England go,

Yet when this fiery web is spun,
   Her watchmen shall descry from far
The young Republic like a sun
   Rise from these crimson seas of war.

To Milton

Milton! I think thy spirit hath passed away
From these white cliffs and high-embattled towers;
   This gorgeous fiery-coloured world of ours
Seems fallen into ashes dull and grey,
And the age changed unto a mimic play
    Wherein we waste our else too-crowded hours:
    For all our pomp and pageantry and powers
We are but fit to delve the common clay,
Seeing this little isle on which we stand,
   This England, this sea-lion of the sea,
   By ignorant demagogues is held in fee,
Who love her not: Dear God! is this the land
    Which bare a triple empire in her hand
    When Cromwell spake the word Democracy!

Louis Napoleon [5]

Eagle of Austerlitz! [6] where were thy wings
    When far away upon a barbarous strand,
    In fight unequal, by an obscure hand,
Fell the last scion of thy brood of Kings!

Poor boy! thou shalt not flaunt thy cloak of red,
    Or ride in state through Paris in the van
    Of thy returning legions, but instead
Thy mother France, free and republican,

Shall on thy dead and crownless forehead place
    The better laurels of a soldier's crown,
    That not dishonoured should thy soul go down
To tell the mighty Sire of thy race

That France hath kissed the mouth of Liberty,
    And found it sweeter than his honied bees,
    And that the giant wave Democracy
Breaks on the shores where Kings lay crouched at ease.

Sonnet
On the Massacre of the Christians in Bulgaria[7]

Christ, dost thou live indeed? or are thy bones
Still straitened in their rock-hewn sepulchre?
And was thy Rising only dreamed by Her
Whose love of thee for all her sin atones?
For here the air is horrid with men's groans,
The priests who call upon thy name are slain,
Dost thou not hear the bitter wail of pain
From those whose children lie upon the stones?
Come down, O Son of God! incestuous gloom
Curtains the land, and through the starless night
Over thy Cross a Crescent moon[8] I see!
If thou in very truth didst burst the tomb
Come down, O Son of Man! and show thy might,
Lest Mahomet be crowned instead of Thee!

Quantum Mutata[9]

There was a time in Europe long ago
When no man died for freedom anywhere,
   But England's lion leaping from its lair
Laid hands on the oppressor! it was so
While England could a great Republic show.
   Witness the men of Piedmont, chiefest care
   Of Cromwell, when with impotent despair
The Pontiff in his painted portico
Trembled before our stern ambassadors.
   How comes it then that from such high estate
   We have thus fallen, save that Luxury
With barren merchandise piles up the gate
Where noble thoughts and deeds should enter by:
   Else might we still be Milton's heritors.

Libertatis Sacra Fames[10]

Albeit nurtured in democracy,
   And liking best that state republican
   Where every man is Kinglike and no man
Is crowned above his fellows, yet I see,
Spite of this modern fret for Liberty,
   Better the rule of One, whom all obey,
   Than to let clamorous demagogues betray
Our freedom with the kiss of anarchy.[11]
Wherefore I love them not whose hands profane
   Plant the red flag upon the piled-up street
   For no right cause, beneath whose ignorant reign
Arts, Culture, Reverence, Honour, all things fade,
   Save Treason and the dagger of her trade,
   Or Murder with his silent bloody feet.

Theoretikos[12]

This mighty empire hath but feet of clay:
   Of all its ancient chivalry and might
   Our little island is forsaken quite:
Some enemy hath stolen its crown of bay,
And from its hills that voice hath passed away
   Which spake of Freedom: O come out of it,
   Come out of it, my Soul, thou art not fit
For this vile traffic-house, where day by day
   Wisdom and reverence are sold at mart,
   And the rude people rage with ignorant cries
Against an heritage of centuries.
   It mars my calm: wherefore in dreams of Art
   And loftiest culture I would stand apart,
Neither for God, nor for his enemies.

THE GARDEN OF EROS

The Garden of Eros

It is full summer now, the heart of June;
   Not yet the sunburnt reapers are astir
Upon the upland meadow where too soon
   Rich autumn time, the season's usurer,
Will lend his hoarded gold to all the trees,
And see his treasure scattered by the wild and spendthrift
    breeze.

Too soon indeed! yet here the daffodil,
   That love-child of the Spring, has lingered on
To vex the rose with jealousy, and still
   The harebell spreads her azure pavilion,
And like a strayed and wandering reveller
Abandoned of its brothers, whom long since June's messenger

The missel-thrush has frighted from the glade,
   One pale narcissus loiters fearfully
Close to a shadowy nook, where half afraid
   Of their own loveliness some violets lie
That will not look the gold sun in the face
For fear of too much splendour, – ah! methinks it is a place

Which should be trodden by Persephone
   When wearied of the flowerless fields of Dis!
Or danced on by the lads of Arcady!
   The hidden secret of eternal bliss
Known to the Grecian here a man might find,
Ah! you and I may find it now if Love and Sleep be kind.

There are the flowers which mourning Herakles
   Strewed on the tomb of Hylas, columbine,
Its white doves all a-flutter where the breeze
   Kissed them too harshly, the small celandine,
That yellow-kirtled chorister of eve,
And lilac lady's-smock, – but let them bloom alone, and leave

Yon spirèd hollyhock red-crocketed
   To sway its silent chimes, else must the bee,
Its little bellringer, go seek instead
   Some other pleasaunce; the anemone
That weeps at daybreak, like a silly girl
Before her love, and hardly lets the butterflies unfurl

Their painted wings beside it, – bid it pine
   In pale virginity; the winter snow
Will suit it better than those lips of thine
   Whose fires would but scorch it, rather go
And pluck that amorous flower which blooms alone,
Fed by the pander wind with dust of kisses not its own.

The trumpet-mouths of red convolvulus
   So dear to maidens, creamy meadow-sweet
Whiter than Juno's throat and odorous
   As all Arabia, hyacinths the feet
Of Huntress Dian would be loth to mar
For any dappled fawn, – pluck these, and those fond flowers
     which are

Fairer than what Queen Venus trod upon
   Beneath the pines of Ida, eucharis,
That morning star which does not dread the sun,
   And budding marjoram which but to kiss
Would sweeten Cytheraea's lips and make
Adonis jealous, – these for thy head, – and for thy girdle take

Yon curving spray of purple clematis
   Whose gorgeous dye outflames the Tyrian King,
And foxgloves with their nodding chalices,
   But that one narciss which the startled Spring
Let from her kirtle fall when first she heard
In her own woods the wild tempestuous song of summer's bird,

Ah! leave it for a subtle memory
   Of those sweet tremulous days of rain and sun,
When April laughed between her tears to see
   The early primrose with shy footsteps run
From the gnarled oak-tree roots till all the wold,
Spite of its brown and trampled leaves, grew bright with
     shimmering gold.

Nay, pluck it too, it is not half so sweet
   As thou thyself, my soul's idolatry!
And when thou art a-wearied at thy feet
   Shall oxlips weave their brightest tapestry,
For thee the woodbine shall forget its pride
And veil its tangled whorls, and thou shalt walk
   on daisies pied.

And I will cut a reed by yonder spring
   And make the wood-gods jealous, and old Pan
Wonder what young intruder dares to sing
   In these still haunts, where never foot of man
Should tread at evening, lest he chance to spy
The marble limbs of Artemis and all her company.

And I will tell thee why the jacinth wears
   Such dread embroidery of dolorous moan,
And why the hapless nightingale forbears
   To sing her song at noon, but weeps alone
When the fleet swallow sleeps, and rich men feast,
And why the laurel trembles when she sees the lightening east.

And I will sing how sad Proserpina
   Unto a grave and gloomy Lord[13] was wed,
And lure the silver-breasted Helena
   Back from the lotus meadows of the dead,
So shalt thou see that awful loveliness
For which two mighty Hosts met fearfully in war's abyss!

And then I'll pipe to thee that Grecian tale
   How Cynthia loves the lad Endymion,
And hidden in a grey and misty veil
   Hies to the cliffs of Latmos once the Sun
Leaps from his ocean bed in fruitless chase
Of those pale flying feet which fade away in his embrace.

And if my flute can breathe sweet melody,
   We may behold Her face who long ago
Dwelt among men by the Aegean sea,
   And whose sad house with pillaged portico
And friezeless wall and columns toppled down
Looms o'er the ruins of that fair and violet cinctured town.

Spirit of Beauty! tarry still awhile,
    They are not dead, thine ancient votaries;
Some few there are to whom thy radiant smile
    Is better than a thousand victories,
Though all the nobly slain of Waterloo
Rise up in wrath against them! tarry still, there are a few

Who for thy sake would give their manlihood
    And consecrate their being; I at least
Have done so, made thy lips my daily food,
    And in thy temples found a goodlier feast
Than this starved age can give me, spite of all
Its new-found creeds so sceptical and so dogmatical.

Here not Cephissos, not Ilissos flows,
    The woods of white Colonos are not here,
On our bleak hills the olive never blows,
    No simple priest conducts his lowing steer
Up the steep marble way, nor through the town
Do laughing maidens bear to thee the crocus-flowered gown.

Yet tarry! for the boy who loved thee best,[14]
    Whose very name should be a memory
To make thee linger, sleeps in silent rest
    Beneath the Roman walls, and melody
Still mourns her sweetest lyre; none can play
The lute of Adonais: with his lips Song passed away.

Nay, when Keats died the Muses still had left
    One silver voice to sing his threnody,
But ah! too soon of it we were bereft
    When on that riven night and stormy sea
Panthea claimed her singer as her own,
And slew the mouth that praised her; since which time we
    walk alone,

Save for that fiery heart, that morning star
    Of re-arisen England, whose clear eye
Saw from our tottering throne and waste of war
    The grand Greek limbs of young Democracy
Rise mightily like Hesperus and bring
The great Republic! him at least thy love hath taught to sing,[15]

And he hath been with thee at Thessaly,
    And seen white Atalanta fleet of foot
In passionless and fierce virginity
    Hunting the tuskèd boar, his honied lute
Hath pierced the cavern of the hollow hill,
And Venus laughs to know one knee will bow before her still.

And he hath kissed the lips of Proserpine,
    And sung the Galilaean's[16] requiem,
That wounded forehead dashed with blood and wine
    He hath discrowned, the Ancient Gods in him
Have found their last, most ardent worshipper,
And the new Sign grows grey and dim before its conqueror.

Spirit of Beauty! tarry with us still,
    It is not quenched the torch of poesy,
The star that shook above the Eastern hill
    Holds unassailed its argent armoury
From all the gathering gloom and fretful fight –
O tarry with us still! for through the long and common night,

Morris, our sweet and simple Chaucer's child,
    Dear heritor of Spenser's tuneful reed,
With soft and sylvan pipe has oft beguiled
    The weary soul of man in troublous need,
And from the far and flowerless fields of ice
Has brought fair flowers to make an earthly paradise.[17]

We know them all, Gudrun the strong men's bride,
    Aslaug and Olafson we know them all,
How giant Grettir fought and Sigurd died,
    And what enchantment held the king in thrall
When lonely Brynhild wrestled with the powers
That war against all passion, ah! how oft through summer hours,

Long listless summer hours when the noon
    Being enamoured of a damask rose
Forgets to journey westward, till the moon
    The pale usurper of its tribute grows
From a thin sickle to a silver shield
And chides its loitering car – how oft, in some cool grassy
    field

Far from the cricket-ground and noisy eight,[18]
    At Bagley,[19] where the rustling bluebells come
Almost before the blackbird finds a mate
    And overstay the swallow, and the hum
Of many murmuring bees flits through the leaves,
Have I lain poring on the dreamy tales his fancy weaves,

And through their unreal woes and mimic pain
    Wept for myself, and so was purified,
And in their simple mirth grew glad again;
    For as I sailed upon that pictured tide
The strength and splendour of the storm was mine
Without the storm's red ruin, for the singer is divine;

The little laugh of water falling down
    Is not so musical, the clammy gold
Close hoarded in the tiny waxen town
    Has less of sweetness in it, and the old
Half-withered reeds that waved in Arcady
Touched by his lips break forth again to fresher harmony.

Spirit of Beauty, tarry yet awhile!
    Although the cheating merchants of the mart
With iron roads profane our lovely isle,
    And break on whirling wheels the limbs of Art,
Ay! though the crowded factories beget
The blindworm Ignorance that slays the soul, O tarry yet!

For One at least there is, – He bears his name
    From Dante and the seraph Gabriel,[20] –
Whose double laurels burn with deathless flame
    To light thine altar; He too loves thee well,
Who saw old Merlin lured in Vivien's snare,
And the white feet of angels coming down the golden stair,

Loves thee so well, that all the World for him
    A gorgeous-coloured vestiture must wear,
And Sorrow take a purple diadem,
    Or else be no more Sorrow, and Despair
Gild its own thorns and Pain, like Adon, be
Even in anguish beautiful; – such is the empery

Which Painters hold, and such the heritage
   This gentle solemn Spirit doth possess,
Being a better mirror of his age
   In all his pity, love, and weariness,
Than those who can but copy common things,
And leave the Soul unpainted with its mighty questionings.

But they are few, and all romance has flown,
   And men can prophesy about the sun,
And lecture on his arrows – how, alone,
   Through a waste void the soulless atoms run,
How from each tree its weeping nymph has fled,
And that no more 'mid English reeds a Naiad shows her head.

Methinks these new Actaeons boast too soon
   That they have spied on beauty; what if we
Have analysed the rainbow, robbed the moon
   Of her most ancient, chastest mystery,
Shall I, the last Endymion, lose all hope
Because rude eyes peer at my mistress through a telescope!

What profit if this scientific age
   Burst through our gates with all its retinue
Of modern miracles! Can it assuage
   One lover's breaking heart? what can it do
To make one life more beautiful, one day
More godlike in its period? but now the Age of Clay

Returns in horrid cycle, and the earth
   Hath borne again a noisy progeny
Of ignorant Titans, whose ungodly birth
   Hurls them against the august hierarchy
Which sat upon Olympus; to the Dust
They have appealed, and to that barren arbiter they must

Repair for judgment; let them, if they can,
   From Natural Warfare and insensate Chance,
Create the new Ideal rule for man!
   Methinks that was not my inheritance;
For I was nurtured otherwise, my soul
Passes from higher heights of life to a more supreme goal.

Lo! while we spake the earth did turn away
  Her visage from the God, and Hecate's boat
Rose silver-laden, till the jealous day
  Blew all its torches out: I did not note
The waning hours, to young Endymions
Time's palsied fingers count in vain his rosary of suns!

Mark how the yellow iris wearily
  Leans back its throat, as though it would be kissed
By its false chamberer, the dragon-fly,
  Who, like a blue vein on a girl's white wrist,
Sleeps on that snowy primrose of the night,
Which 'gins to flush with crimson shame, and die beneath
  the light.

Come let us go, against the pallid shield
  Of the wan sky the almond blossoms gleam,
The corncrake nested in the unmown field
  Answers its mate, across the misty stream
On fitful wing the startled curlews fly,
And in his sedgy bed the lark, for joy that Day is nigh,

Scatters the pearlèd dew from off the grass,
  In tremulous ecstasy to greet the sun,
Who soon in gilded panoply will pass
  Forth from yon orange-curtained pavilion
Hung in the burning east: see, the red rim
O'ertops the expectant hills! it is the God! for love of him

Already the shrill lark is out of sight,
  Flooding with waves of song this silent dell, –
Ah! there is something more in that bird's flight
  Than could be tested in a crucible! –
But the air freshens, let us go, why soon
The woodmen will be here; how we have lived this night
  of June!

ROSA MYSTICA[21]

Requiescat[22]

Tread lightly, she is near
   Under the snow,
Speak gently, she can hear
   The daisies grow.

All her bright golden hair
   Tarnished with rust,
She that was young and fair
   Fallen to dust.

Lily-like, white as snow,
   She hardly knew
She was a woman, so
   Sweetly she grew.

Coffin-board, heavy stone,
   Lie on her breast,
I vex my heart alone,
   She is at rest.

Peace, Peace, she cannot hear
   Lyre or sonnet,
All my life's buried here,
   Heap earth upon it.

                        AVIGNON

Sonnet on Approaching Italy

I reached the Alps: the soul within me burned,
   Italia, my Italia, at thy name:
   And when from out the mountain's heart I came
And saw the land for which my life had yearned,
I laughed as one who some great prize had earned:
   And musing on the marvel of thy fame
   I watched the day, till marked with wounds of flame
The turquoise sky to burnished gold was turned.
The pine-trees waved as waves a woman's hair,
   And in the orchards every twining spray
   Was breaking into flakes of blossoming foam:
But when I knew that far away at Rome
   In evil bonds a second Peter[23] lay,
   I wept to see the land so very fair.

                         TURIN

San Miniato[24]

   See, I have climbed the mountain side
   Up to this holy house of God,
   Where once that Angel-Painter[25] trod
Who saw the heavens opened wide,

   And throned upon the crescent moon
   The Virginal white Queen of Grace, –
   Mary! could I but see thy face
Death could not come at all too soon.

   O crowned by God with thorns and pain!
   Mother of Christ! O mystic wife!
   My heart is weary of this life
And over-sad to sing again.

   O crowned by God with love and flame!
   O crowned by Christ the Holy One!
   O listen ere the searching sun
Show to the world my sin and shame.

Ave Maria Gratia Plena[26]

Was this His coming! I had hoped to see
  A scene of wondrous glory, as was told
  Of some great God who in a rain of gold
Broke open bars and fell on Danae:
Or a dread vision as when Semele
  Sickening for love and unappeased desire
  Prayed to see God's clear body, and the fire
Caught her brown limbs and slew her utterly:
With such glad dreams I sought this holy place,
  And now with wondering eyes and heart I stand
  Before this supreme mystery of Love:
Some kneeling girl with passionless pale face,
  An angel with a lily in his hand,
  And over both the white wings of a Dove.

                           FLORENCE

Italia

Italia! thou art fallen, though with sheen
  Of battle-spears thy clamorous armies stride
  From the north Alps to the Sicilian tide!
Ay! fallen, though the nations hail thee Queen
Because rich gold in every town is seen,
  And on thy sapphire-lake in tossing pride
  Of wind-filled vans thy myriad galleys ride
Beneath one flag of red and white and green.
O Fair and Strong! O Strong and Fair in vain!
  Look southward where Rome's desecrated town
  Lies mourning for her God-anointed King!
Look heaven-ward! shall God allow this thing?
  Nay! but some flame-girt Raphael shall come down,
  And smite the Spoiler with the sword of pain.

                              VENICE

Sonnet
Written in Holy Week at Genoa

I wandered through Scoglietto's far retreat,
    The oranges on each o'erhanging spray
    Burned as bright lamps of gold to shame the day;
Some startled bird with fluttering wings and fleet
Made snow of all the blossoms; at my feet
    Like silver moons the pale narcissi lay:
    And the curved waves that streaked the great green bay
Laughed i' the sun, and life seemed very sweet.
Outside the young boy-priest passed singing clear,
    'Jesus the son of Mary has been slain,
    O come and fill his sepulchre with flowers.'
Ah, God! Ah, God! those dear Hellenic hours
    Had drowned all memory of Thy bitter pain,
    The Cross, the Crown, the Soldiers and the Spear.

Rome Unvisited

I

The corn has turned from grey to red,
    Since first my spirit wandered forth,
    From the drear cities of the north,
And to Italia's mountains fled.

And here I set my face towards home,
    For all my pilgrimage is done,
    Although, methinks, yon blood-red sun
Marshals the way to Holy Rome.

O Blessed Lady, who dost hold
    Upon the seven hills thy reign!
    O Mother without blot or stain,
Crowned with bright crowns of triple gold!

O Roma, Roma, at thy feet
I lay this barren gift of song!
    For, ah! the way is steep and long
That leads unto thy sacred street.

II

And yet what joy it were for me
    To turn my feet unto the south,
    And journeying towards the Tiber mouth
To kneel again at Fiesole!

And wandering through the tangled pines
    That break the gold of Arno's stream,
    To see the purple mist and gleam
Of morning on the Apennines.

By many a vineyard-hidden home,
    Orchard and olive-garden grey,
    Till from the drear Campagna's way
The seven hills bear up the dome!

III

A Pilgrim from the northern seas –
    What joy for me to seek alone
    The wondrous Temple and the throne
Of Him who holds the awful keys!

When, bright with purple and with gold,
    Come priest and holy Cardinal,
    And borne above the heads of all
The gentle Shepherd of the Fold.

O joy to see before I die
    The only God-anointed King,
    And hear the silver trumpets ring
A triumph as He passes by!

Or at the brazen-pillared shrine
    Holds high the mystic sacrifice,
    And shows his God to human eyes
Beneath the veil of bread and wine.

IV

For lo, what changes time can bring!
    The cycles of revolving years
    May free my heart from all its fears,
And teach my lips a song to sing.

Before yon field of trembling gold
    Is garnered into dusty sheaves,
    Or ere the autumn's scarlet leaves
Flutter as birds adown the wold,

I may have run the glorious race,
    And caught the torch while yet aflame,
    And called upon the holy name
Of Him who now doth hide His face.

ARONA

Urbs Sacra Aeterna[27]

Rome! what a scroll of History thine has been;
    In the first days thy sword republican
    Ruled the whole world for many an age's span:
Then of the peoples wert thou royal Queen,
Till in thy streets the bearded Goth was seen;
    And now upon thy walls the breezes fan
    (Ah, city crowned by God, discrowned by man!)
The hated flag of red and white and green.
When was thy glory! when in search for power
    Thine eagles flew to greet the double sun,
    And the wild nations shuddered at thy rod?
Nay, but thy glory tarried for this hour,
    When pilgrims kneel before the Holy One,
    The prisoned shepherd[28] of the Church of God.

MONTE MARIO

Sonnet
On hearing the Dies Irae in the Sistine Chapel

Nay, Lord, not thus! white lilies in the spring,
Sad olive-groves, or silver-breasted dove,
   Teach me more clearly of Thy life and love
Than terrors of red flame and thundering.
The hillside vines dear memories of Thee bring:
   A bird at evening flying to its nest
   Tells me of One who had no place of rest:
I think it is of Thee the sparrows sing.
Come rather on some autumn afternoon,
   When red and brown are burnished on the leaves,
   And the fields echo to the gleaner's song,
Come when the splendid fulness of the moon
   Looks down upon the rows of golden sheaves,
   And reap Thy harvest: we have waited long.

Easter Day

The silver trumpets rang across the Dome:
   The people knelt upon the ground with awe:
   And borne upon the necks of men I saw,
Like some great God, the Holy Lord of Rome.
Priest-like, he wore a robe more white than foam,
   And, king-like, swathed himself in royal red,
   Three crowns of gold[29] rose high upon his head:
In splendour and in light the Pope passed home.
My heart stole back across wide wastes of years
   To one who wandered[30] by a lonely sea,
   And sought in vain for any place of rest:
'Foxes have holes, and every bird its nest.
   I, only I, must wander wearily,
   And bruise my feet, and drink wine salt with tears.'

E Tenebris[31]

Come down, O Christ, and help me! reach thy hand,
    For I am drowning in a stormier sea
    Than Simon on thy lake of Galilee:
The wine of life is spilt upon the sand,
My heart is as some famine-murdered land
    Whence all good things have perished utterly,
    And well I know my soul in Hell must lie
If I this night before God's throne should stand.
'He sleeps perchance, or rideth to the chase,
    Like Baal, when his prophets howled that name
    From morn to noon on Carmel's smitten height.'
Nay, peace, I shall behold, before the night,
    The feet of brass, the robe more white than flame,
    The wounded hands, the weary human face.

Vita Nuova[32]

I stood by the unvintageable sea[33]
    Till the wet waves drenched face and hair with spray;
    The long red fires of the dying day
Burned in the west; the wind piped drearily;
And to the land the clamorous gulls did flee:
    'Alas!' I cried, 'my life is full of pain,
    And who can garner fruit or golden grain
From these waste fields which travail ceaselessly!'
My nets gaped wide with many a break and flaw,
    Nathless I threw them as my final cast[34]
    Into the sea, and waited for the end.
When lo! a sudden glory! and I saw
    From the black waters of my tortured past
    The argent splendour of white limbs ascend![35]

Madonna Mia[36]

A lily-girl,[37] not made for this world's pain,
   With brown, soft hair close braided by her ears,
   And longing eyes half veiled by slumberous tears
Like bluest water seen through mists of rain:
Pale cheeks whereon no love hath left its stain,
   Red underlip drawn in for fear of love,
   And white throat, whiter than the silvered dove,
Through whose wan marble creeps one purple vein.
Yet, though my lips shall praise her without cease,
   Even to kiss her feet I am not bold,
   Being o'ershadowed by the wings of awe,
Like Dante, when he stood with Beatrice
   Beneath the flaming Lion's breast, and saw
   The seventh Crystal, and the Stair of Gold.

The New Helen

Where hast thou been since round the walls of Troy
   The sons of God fought in that great emprise?
    Why dost thou walk our common earth again?
Hast thou forgotten that impassioned boy,
    His purple galley and his Tyrian men
   And treacherous Aphrodite's mocking eyes?
For surely it was thou, who, like a star
   Hung in the silver silence of the night,
   Didst lure the Old World's chivalry and might
Into the clamorous crimson waves of war!

Or didst thou rule the fire-laden moon?
   In amorous Sidon was thy temple built
    Over the light and laughter of the sea
Where, behind lattice scarlet-wrought and gilt,
    Some brown-limbed girl did weave thee tapestry,
   All through the waste and wearied hours of noon;
Till her wan cheek with flame of passion burned,
   And she rose up the sea-washed lips to kiss
   Of some glad Cyprian sailor, safe returned
From Calpé and the cliffs of Herakles!

No! thou art Helen, and none other one!
   It was for thee that young Sarpedôn died,
      And Memnôn's manhood was untimely spent;
   It was for thee gold-crested Hector tried
With Thetis' child[38] that evil race to run,
      In the last year of thy beleaguerment;
Ay! even now the glory of thy fame
   Burns in those fields of trampled asphodel,
   Where the high lords whom Ilion knew so well
Clash ghostly shields, and call upon thy name.

Where hast thou been? in that enchanted land
   Whose slumbering vales forlorn Calypso knew,
      Where never mower rose at break of day
   But all unswathed the trammelling grasses grew,
And the sad shepherd saw the tall corn stand
      Till summer's red had changed to withered grey?
Didst thou lie there by some Lethaean stream
   Deep brooding on thine ancient memory,
The crash of broken spears, the fiery gleam
   From shivered helm, the Grecian battle-cry?

Nay, thou wert hidden in that hollow hill
   With one who is forgotten utterly,
      That discrowned Queen men call the Erycine;
   Hidden away that never mightst thou see
      The face of Her, before whose mouldering shrine
Today at Rome the silent nations kneel;
   Who gat from Love no joyous gladdening,
      But only Love's intolerable pain,
      Only a sword to pierce her heart in twain,
Only the bitterness of child-bearing.

The lotus-leaves which heal the wounds of Death
   Lie in thy hand; O, be thou kind to me,
      While yet I know the summer of my days;
For hardly can my tremulous lips draw breath
      To fill the silver trumpet with thy praise,
   So bowed am I before thy mystery;
So bowed and broken on Love's terrible wheel,

That I have lost all hope and heart to sing,
    Yet care I not what ruin time may bring
If in thy temple thou wilt let me kneel.

Alas, alas, thou wilt not tarry here,
    But, like that bird, the servant of the sun
        Who flies before the north wind and the night,
So wilt thou fly our evil land and drear,
        Back to the tower of thine old delight,
    And the red lips of young Euphorion;
Nor shall I ever see thy face again,
    But in this poisonous garden-close must stay,
Crowning my brows with the thorn-crown of pain,
    Till all my loveless life shall pass away.

O Helen! Helen! Helen! yet a while,
    Yet for a little while, O, tarry here,
        Till the dawn cometh and the shadows flee!
For in the gladsome sunlight of thy smile
    Of heaven or hell I have no thought or fear
        Seeing I know no other god but thee:
No other god save him, before whose feet
    In nets of gold the tired planets move,
    The incarnate spirit of spiritual love
Who in thy body holds his joyous seat.

Thou wert not born as common women are!
    But, girt with silver splendour of the foam,
        Didst from the depths of sapphire seas arise!
And at thy coming some immortal star,
        Bearded with flame, blazed in the Eastern skies,
    And waked the shepherds on thine island-home.
Thou shalt not die: no asps of Egypt creep
    Close at thy heels to taint the delicate air;
    No sullen-blooming poppies stain thy hail,
Those scarlet heralds of eternal sleep.

Lily of love, pure and inviolate!
   Tower of ivory! red rose of fire!
      Thou hast come down our darkness to illume:
For we, close-caught in the wide nets of Fate,
   Wearied with waiting for the World's Desire,
      Aimlessly wandered in the House of gloom,
Aimlessly sought some slumberous anodyne
   For wasted lives, for lingering wretchedness,
Till we beheld thy re-arisen shrine,
   And the white glory of thy loveliness.

THE BURDEN OF ITYS

The Burden of Itys

This English Thames is holier far than Rome,
    Those harebells like a sudden flush of sea
Breaking across the woodland, with the foam
    Of meadow-sweet and white anemone
To fleck their blue waves, – God is likelier there
Than hidden in that crystal-hearted star the pale monks bear!

Those violet-gleaming butterflies that take
    Yon creamy lily for their pavilion
Are monsignores, and where the rushes shake
    A lazy pike lies basking in the sun,
His eyes half shut, – he is some mitred old
Bishop *in partibus*! look at those gaudy scales all green and
    gold.

The wind the restless prisoner of the trees
    Does well for Palaestrina, one would say
The mighty master's hands were on the keys
    Of the Maria organ, which they play
When early on some sapphire Easter morn
In a high litter red as blood or sin the Pope is borne

From his dark House out to the Balcony
    Above the bronze gates and the crowded square,
Whose very fountains seem for ecstasy
    To toss their silver lances in the air,
And stretching out weak hands to East and West
In vain sends peace to peaceless lands, to restless nations rest.

Is not yon lingering orange after-glow
    That stays to vex the moon more fair than all
Rome's lordliest pageants! strange, a year ago
        I knelt before some crimson Cardinal
        Who bare the Host across the Esquiline,
        And now – those common poppies in the wheat seem twice
            as fine.

The blue-green beanfields yonder, tremulous
  With the last shower, sweeter perfume bring
Through this cool evening than the odorous
  Flame-jewelled censers the young deacons swing,
When the grey priest unlocks the curtained shrine,
And makes God's body from the common fruit of corn and
    vine.

Poor Fra Giovanni bawling at the mass
  Were out of tune now, for a small brown bird
Sings overhead, and through the long cool grass
  I see that throbbing throat which once heard
On starlit hills of flower-starred Arcady,
Once where the white and crescent sand of Salamis meets sea.

Sweet is the swallow twittering on the eaves
  At daybreak, when the mower whets his scythe,
And stock-doves murmur, and the milkmaid leaves
  Her little lonely bed, and carols blithe
To see the heavy-lowing cattle wait
Stretching their huge and dripping mouths across the
    farmyard gate.

And sweet the hops upon the Kentish leas,
  And sweet the wind that lifts the new-mown hay,
And sweet the fretful swarms of grumbling bees
  That round and round the linden blossoms play;
And sweet the heifer breathing in the stall,
And the green bursting figs that hang upon the red-brick wall.

And sweet to hear the cuckoo mock the spring
  While the last violet loiters by the well,
And sweet to hear the shepherd Daphnis sing
  The song of Linus through a sunny dell
Of warm Arcadia where the corn is gold
And the slight lithe-limbed reapers dance about the wattled
    fold.

And sweet with young Lycoris to recline
   In some Illyrian valley far away,
Where canopied on herbs amaracine
   We too might waste the summer-trancèd day
Matching our reeds in sportive rivalry,
While far beneath us frets the troubled purple of the sea.

But sweeter far if silver-sandalled foot
   Of some long-hidden God should ever tread
The Nuneham[39] meadows, if with reeded flute
   Pressed to his lips some Faun might raise his head
By the green water-flags, ah! sweet indeed
To see the heavenly herdsman call his white-fleeced flock
     to feed.

Then sing to me thou tuneful chorister,
   Though what thou sing'st be thine own requiem!
Tell me thy tale thou hapless chronicler
   Of thine own tragedies! do not contemn
These unfamiliar haunts, this English field,
For many a lovely coronal our northern isle can yield

Which Grecian meadows know not, many a rose
   Which all day long in vales Aeolian
A lad might seek in vain for over-grows
   Our hedges like a wanton courtesan
Unthrifty of its beauty; lilies too
Ilissos never mirrored star our streams, and cockles blue

Dot the green wheat which, though they are the signs
   For swallows going south, would never spread
Their azure tents between the Attic vines;
   Even that little weed of ragged red,
Which bids the robin pipe, in Arcady
Would be a trespasser, and many an unsung elegy

Sleeps in the reeds that fringe our winding Thames
   Which to awake were sweeter ravishment
Than ever Syrinx wept for; diadems
   Of brown bee-studded orchids which were meant

For Cytheraea's brows are hidden here
Unknown to Cytheraea, and by yonder pasturing steer

There is a tiny yellow daffodil,
    The butterfly can see it from afar,
Although one summer evening's dew could fill
    Its little cup twice over ere the star
Had called the lazy shepherd to his fold
And be no prodigal; each leaf is flecked with spotted gold

As if Jove's gorgeous leman Danae
    Hot from his gilded arms had stooped to kiss
The trembling petals, or young Mercury
    Low-flying to the dusky ford of Dis
Had with one feather of his pinions
Just brushed them! the slight stem which bears the burden of
        its suns

Is hardly thicker than the gossamer,
    Or poor Arachne's silver tapestry, –
Men say it bloomed upon the sepulchre
    Of One I sometime worshipped, but to me
It seems to bring diviner memories
Of faun-loved Heliconian glades and blue nymph-haunted
        seas,

Of an untrodden vale at Tempe where
    On the clear river's marge Narcissus lies,
The tangle of the forest in his hair,
    The silence of the woodland in his eyes,
Wooing that drifting imagery which is
No sooner kissed than broken; memories of Salmacis

Who is not boy nor girl and yet is both,
    Fed by two fires and unsatisfied
Through their excess, each passion being loth
    For love's own sake to leave the other's side
Yet killing love by staying; memories
Of Oreads peeping through the leaves of silent moonlit trees,

Of lonely Ariadne on the wharf
   At Naxos, when she saw the treacherous crew
Far out at sea, and waved her crimson scarf
   And called false Theseus back again nor knew
That Dionysos on an amber pard
Was close behind her; memories of what Maeonia's bard [40]

With sightless eyes beheld, the wall of Troy,
   Queen Helen lying in the ivory room,
And at her side an amorous red-lipped boy
   Trimming with dainty hand his helmet's plume,
And far away the moil, the shout, the groan,
As Hector shielded off the spear and Ajax hurled the stone;

Of wingèd Perseus with his flawless sword
   Cleaving the snaky tresses of the witch,
And all those tales imperishably stored
   In little Grecian urns, freightage more rich
Than any gaudy galleon of Spain
Bare from the Indies ever! these at least bring back again,

For well I know they are not dead at all,
   The ancient Gods of Grecian poesy:
They are asleep, and when they hear thee call
   Will wake and think 'tis very Thessaly,
This Thames the Daulian waters, this cool glade
The yellow-irised mead where once young Itys laughed and
     played.

If it was thou dear jasmine-cradled bird
   Who from the leafy stillness of thy throne
Sang to the wondrous boy, until he heard
   The horn of Atalanta [41] faintly blown
Across the Cumnor hills, and wandering
Through Bagley wood [42] at evening found the Attic poets'
     spring, –

Ah! tiny sober-suited advocate
   That pleadest for the moon against the day!
If thou didst make the shepherd seek his mate

On that sweet questing, when Proserpina
Forgot it was not Sicily and leant
Across the mossy Sandford stile in ravished wonderment, –

Light-winged and bright-eyed miracle of the wood!
    If ever thou didst soothe with melody
One of that little clan, that brotherhood [43]
    Which loved the morning-star of Tuscany
More than the perfect sun of Raphael
And is immortal, sing to me! for I too love thee well.

Sing on! sing on! let the dull world grow young,
    Let elemental things take form again,
And the old shapes of Beauty walk among
    The simple garths and open crofts, as when
The son of Leto [44] bare the willow rod,
And the soft sheep and shaggy goats followed the boyish God.

Sing on! sing on! and Bacchus will be here
    Astride upon his gorgeous Indian throne,
And over whimpering tigers shake the spear
    With yellow ivy crowned and gummy cone,
While at his side the wanton Bassarid
Will throw the lion by the mane and catch the mountain kid!

Sing on! and I will wear the leopard skin,
    And steal the mooned wings of Ashtaroth,
Upon whose icy chariot we could win
    Cithaeron in an hour ere the froth
Has over-brimmed the wine-vat or the Faun
Ceased from the treading! ay, before the flickering lamp of
    dawn

Has scared the hooting owlet to its nest,
    And warned the bat to close its filmy vans,
Some Maenad girl with vine-leaves on her breast
    Will filch their beech-nuts from the sleeping Pans
So softly that the little nested thrush
Will never wake, and then with shrilly laugh and leap will rush

Down the green valley where the fallen dew
   Lies thick beneath the elm and count her store,
Till the brown Satyrs in a jolly crew
   Trample the loosestrife down along the shore,
And where their hornèd master sits in state
Bring strawberries and bloomy plums upon a wicker crate!

Sing on! and soon with passion-wearied face
   Through the cool leaves Apollo's lad will come,
The Tyrian prince his bristled boar will chase
   Adown the chestnut-copses all a-bloom,
And ivory-limbed, grey-eyed, with look of pride,
After yon velvet-coated deer the virgin maid will ride.

Sing on! and I the dying boy will see
   Stain with his purple blood the waxen bell
That overweighs the jacinth, and to me
   The wretched Cyprian her woe will tell,
And I will kiss her mouth and streaming eyes,
And lead her to the myrtle-hidden grove where Adon lies!

Cry out aloud on Itys! memory
   That foster-brother of remorse and pain
Drops poison in mine ear, – O to be free,
   To burn one's old ships! and to launch again
Into the white-plumed battle of the waves
And fight old Proteus for the spoil of coral-flowered caves!

O for Medea with her poppied spell!
   O for the secret of the Colchian shrine!
O for one leaf of that pale asphodel
   Which binds the tired brows of Proserpine,
And sheds such wondrous dews at eve that she
Dreams of the fields of Enna, by the far Sicilian sea,

Where oft the golden-girdled bee she chased
   From lily to lily on the level mead,
Ere yet her sombre Lord had bid her taste
   The deadly fruit of that pomegranate seed,
Ere the black steeds had harried her away
Down to the faint and flowerless land, the sick and
   sunless day.

O for one midnight and as paramour
   The Venus of the little Melian farm!
O that some antique statue for one hour
   Might wake to passion, and that I could charm
The Dawn at Florence from its dumb despair,
Mix with those mighty limbs and make that giant breast my
    lair!

Sing on! sing on! I would be drunk with life,
   Drunk with the trampled vintage of my youth,
I would forget the wearying wasted strife,
   The riven veil, the Gorgon eyes of Truth,
The prayerless vigil and the cry for prayer,
The barren gifts, the lifted arms, the dull insensate air!

Sing on! sing on! O feathered Niobe,
   Thou canst make sorrow beautiful, and steal
From joy its sweetest music, not as we
   Who by dead voiceless silence strive to heal
Our too untented wounds, and do but keep
Pain barricadoed in our hearts, and murder pillowed sleep.

Sing louder yet, why must I still behold
   The wan white face of that deserted Christ,
Whose bleeding hands my hands did once enfold,
   Whose smitten lips my lips so oft have kissed,
And now in mute and marble misery
Sits in his lone dishonoured House and weeps, perchance for
    me?

O Memory cast down thy wreathèd shell!
   Break thy hoarse lute O sad Melpomene!
O Sorrow, Sorrow keep thy cloistered cell
   Nor dim with tears this limpid Castaly!
Cease, Philomel, thou dost the forest wrong
To vex its sylvan quiet with such wild impassioned song!

Cease, cease, or if 'tis anguish to be dumb
   Take from the pastoral thrush her simpler air,
Whose jocund carelessness doth more become

This English woodland than thy keen despair,
Ah! cease and let the north wind bear thy lay
Back to the rocky hills of Thrace, the stormy Daulian bay.

A moment more, the startled leaves had stirred,
    Endymion would have passed across the mead
Moonstruck with love, and this still Thames had heard
    Pan plash and paddle groping for some reed
To lure from her blue cave that Naiad maid
Who for such piping listens half in joy and half afraid.

A moment more, the waking dove had cooed,
    The silver daughter of the silver sea
With the fond gyves of clinging hands had wooed
    Her wanton from the chase, and Dryope
Had thrust aside the branches of her oak
To see the lusty gold-haired lad rein in his snorting yoke.

A moment more, the trees had stooped to kiss
    Pale Daphne just awakening from the swoon
Of tremulous laurels, lonely Salmacis
    Had bared his barren beauty to the moon,
And through the vale with sad voluptuous smile
Antinous had wandered, the red lotus of the Nile

Down leaning from his black and clustering hair,
    To shade those slumberous eyelids' caverned bliss,
Or else on yonder grassy slope with bare
    High-tuniced limbs unravished Artemis
Had bade her hounds give tongue, and roused the deer
From his green ambuscade with shrill halloo and pricking
        spear.

Lie still, lie still, O passionate heart, lie still!
    O Melancholy, fold thy raven wing!
O sobbing Dryad, from thy hollow hill
    Come not with such despondent answering!
No more thou wingèd Marsyas complain,
Apollo loveth not to hear such troubled songs of pain!

It was a dream, the glade is tenantless,
　　No soft Ionian laughter moves the air,
The Thames creeps on in sluggish leadenness,
　　And from the copse left desolate and bare
Fled is young Bacchus with his revelry,
Yet still from Nuneham wood there comes that thrilling
　　melody

So sad, that one might think a human heart
　　Brake in each separate note, a quality
Which music sometimes has, being the Art
　　Which is most nigh to tears and memory;
Poor mourning Philomel, what dost thou fear?
Thy sister doth not haunt these fields, Pandion is not here,

Here is no cruel Lord with murderous blade,
　　No woven web of bloody heraldries,
But mossy dells for roving comrades made,
　　Warm valleys where the tired student lies
With half-shut book, and many a winding walk
Where rustic lovers stray at eve in happy simple talk.

The harmless rabbit gambols with its young
　　Across the trampled towing-path, where late
A troop of laughing boys in jostling throng
　　Cheered with their noisy cries the racing eight;
The gossamer, with ravelled silver threads,
Works at its little loom, and from the dusky red-eaved sheds

Of the lone Farm a flickering light shines out
　　Where the swinked shepherd drives his bleating flock
Back to their wattled sheep-cotes, a faint shout
　　Comes from some Oxford boat at Sandford lock,
And starts the moor-hen from the sedgy rill,
And the dim lengthening shadows flit like swallows up the hill.

The heron passes homeward to the mere,
　　The blue mist creeps among the shivering trees,
Gold world by world the silent stars appear,
　　And like a blossom blown before the breeze

A white moon drifts across the shimmering sky,
Mute arbitress of all thy sad, thy rapturous threnody.

She does not heed thee, wherefore should she heed,
   She knows Endymion is not far away;
'Tis I, 'tis I, whose soul is as the reed
   Which has no message of its own to play,
So pipes another's bidding, it is I,
Drifting with every wind on the wide sea of misery.

Ah! the brown bird has ceased: one exquisite trill
   About the sombre woodland seems to cling
Dying in music, else the air is still,
   So still that one might hear the bat's small wing
Wander and wheel above the pines, or tell
Each tiny dew-drop dripping from the bluebell's brimming
   cell.

And far away across the lengthening wold,
   Across the willowy flats and thickets brown,
Magdalen's tall tower[45] tipped with tremulous gold
   Marks the long High Street of the little town,
And warns me to return; I must not wait,
Hark! 'tis the curfew booming from the bell at Christ
   Church gate.

WIND FLOWERS

Impression du Matin

The Thames nocturne of blue and gold
    Changed to a Harmony in grey:
    A barge with ochre-coloured hay
Dropt from the wharf: and chill and cold

The yellow fog came creeping down
    The bridges, till the houses' walls
    Seemed changed to shadows and St Paul's
Loomed like a bubble o'er the town.

Then suddenly arose the clang
    Of waking life; the streets were stirred
    With country waggons: and a bird
Flew to the glistening roofs and sang.

But one pale woman all alone,
    The daylight kissing her wan hair,
    Loitered beneath the gas lamps' flare,
With lips of flame and heart of stone.

Magdalen Walks [46]

The little white clouds are racing over the sky,
    And the fields are strewn with the gold of the flower of
      March,
     The daffodil breaks under foot, and the tasselled larch
Sways and swings as the thrush goes hurrying by.

A delicate odour is borne on the wings of the morning breeze,
    The odour of deep wet grass, and of brown new-furrowed
      earth,
     The birds are singing for joy of the Spring's glad birth,
Hopping from branch to branch on the rocking trees.

And all the woods are alive with the murmur and sound of
    Spring,
    And the rose-bud breaks into pink on the climbing briar,
    And the crocus-bed is a quivering moon of fire
Girdled round with the belt of an amethyst ring.

And the plane to the pine-tree is whispering some tale of love
    Till it rustles with laughter and tosses its mantle of green,
    And the gloom of the wych-elm's hollow is lit with the iris
      sheen
Of the burnished rainbow throat and the silver breast of a
    dove.

See! the lark starts up from his bed in the meadow there,
    Breaking the gossamer threads and the nets of dew,
    And flashing adown the river, a flame of blue!
The kingfisher flies like an arrow, and wounds the air.

Athanasia[47]

To that gaunt House of Art[48] which lacks for naught
    Of all the great things men have saved from Time,
The withered body of a girl was brought
    Dead ere the world's glad youth had touched its prime,
And seen by lonely Arabs lying hid
In the dim womb of some black pyramid.

But when they had unloosed the linen band
    Which swathed the Egyptian's body, – lo! was found
Closed in the wasted hollow of her hand
    A little seed, which sown in English ground
Did wondrous snow of starry blossoms bear
And spread rich odours through our spring-tide air.

With such strange arts this flower did allure
    That all forgotten was the asphodel,
And the brown bee, the lily's paramour,
    Forsook the cup where he was wont to dwell,
For not a thing of earth it seemed to be,
But stolen from some heavenly Arcady.

In vain the sad narcissus, wan and white
    At its own beauty, hung across the stream,
The purple dragon-fly had no delight
    With its gold dust to make his wings a-gleam,
Ah! no delight the jasmine-bloom to kiss,
Or brush the rain-pearls from the eucharis.

For love of it the passionate nightingale
    Forgot the hills of Thrace, the cruel king,
And the pale dove no longer cared to sail
    Through the wet woods at time of blossoming,
But round this flower of Egypt sought to float,
With silvered wing and amethystine throat.

While the hot sun blazed in his tower of blue
　A cooling wind crept from the land of snows,
And the warm south with tender tears of dew
　Drenched its white leaves when Hesperos up-rose
Amid those sea-green meadows of the sky
On which the scarlet bars of sunset lie.

But when o'er wastes of lily-haunted field
　The tired birds had stayed their amorous tune,
And broad and glittering like an argent shield
　High in the sapphire heavens hung the moon,
Did no strange dream or evil memory make
Each tremulous petal of its blossoms shake?

Ah no! to this bright flower a thousand years
　Seemed but the lingering of a summer's day,
It never knew the tide of cankering fears
　Which turn a boy's gold hair to withered grey,
The dread desire of death it never knew,
Or how all folk that they were born must rue.

For we to death with pipe and dancing go,
　Nor would we pass the ivory gate again,
As some sad river wearied of its flow
　Through the dull plains, the haunts of common men,
Leaps lover-like into the terrible sea!
And counts it gain to die so gloriously.

We mar our lordly strength in barren strife
　With the world's legions led by clamorous care,
It never feels decay but gathers life
　From the pure sunlight and the supreme air,
We live beneath Time's wasting sovereignty,
It is the child of all eternity.

Serenade
for Music

The western wind is blowing fair
   Across the dark Aegean sea,
And at the secret marble stair
   My Tyrian galley[49] waits for thee.
Come down! the purple sail is spread,
   The watchman sleeps within the town,
O leave thy lily-flowered bed,
   O Lady mine come down, come down!

She will not come, I know her well,
   Of lover's vows she hath no care,
And little good a man can tell
   Of one so cruel and so fair.
True love is but a woman's toy,
   They never know the lover's pain,
And I who loved as loves a boy
   Must love in vain, must love in vain.

O noble pilot, tell me true,
   Is that the sheen of golden hair?
Or is it but the tangled dew
   That binds the passion-flowers there?
Good sailor come and tell me now
   Is that my Lady's lily hand?
Or is it but the gleaming prow,
   Or is it but the silver sand?

No! no! 'tis not the tangled dew,
   'Tis not the silver-fretted sand,
It is my own dear Lady true
   With golden hair and lily hand!
O noble pilot, steer for Troy,
   Good sailor, ply the labouring oar,
This is the Queen of life and joy
   Whom we must bear from Grecian shore!

The waning sky grows faint and blue,
　It wants an hour still of day,
Aboard! aboard! my gallant crew,
　O Lady mine, away! away!
O noble pilot, steer for Troy,
　Good sailor, ply the labouring oar,
O loved as only loves a boy!
　O loved for ever evermore!

Endymion
for Music

The apple trees are hung with gold,
　And birds are loud in Arcady,
The sheep lie bleating in the fold,
The wild goat runs across the wold,
But yesterday his love he told,
　I know he will come back to me.
O rising moon! O Lady moon!
　Be you my lover's sentinel,
　You cannot choose but know him well,
For he is shod with purple shoon,
You cannot choose but know my love,
　For he a shepherd's crook doth bear,
And he is soft as any dove,
　And brown and curly is his hair.

The turtle now has ceased to call
　Upon her crimson-footed groom,
The grey wolf prowls about the stall,
The lily's singing seneschal
Sleeps in the lily-bell, and all
　The violet hills are lost in gloom.
O risen moon! O holy moon!
　Stand on the top of Helice,
　And if my own true love you see,
Ah! if you see the purple shoon,
The hazel crook, the lad's brown hair,
　The goat-skin wrapped about his arm,
Tell him that am waiting where
　The rushlight glimmers in the Farm.

The falling dew is cold and chill,
   And no bird sings in Arcady,
The little fauns have left the hill,
Even the tired daffodil
Has closed its gilded doors, and still
   My lover comes not back to me.
False moon! False moon! O waning moon!
   Where is my own true lover gone,
   Where are the lips vermilion,
The shepherd's crook, the purple shoon?
Why spread that silver pavilion,
   Why wear that veil of drifting mist?
Ah! thou hast young Endymion,
   Thou hast the lips that should be kissed!

La Bella Donna Della Mia Mente [50]

My limbs are wasted with a flame,
   My feet are sore with travelling,
For, calling on my Lady's name,
   My lips have now forgot to sing.

O Linnet in the wild-rose brake
   Strain for my Love thy melody,
O Lark sing louder for love's sake,
   My gentle Lady passeth by.

She is too fair for any man
   To see or hold his heart's delight,
Fairer than Queen or courtesan
   Or moonlit water in the night.

Her hair is bound with myrtle leaves,
   (Green leaves upon her golden hair!)
Green grasses through the yellow sheaves
   Of autumn corn are not more fair.

Her little lips, more made to kiss
   Than to cry bitterly for pain,
Are tremulous as brook-water is,
   Or roses after evening rain.

Her neck is like white melilote
Flushing for pleasure of the sun,
The throbbing of the linnet's throat
Is not so sweet to look upon.

As a pomegranate, cut in twain,
White-seeded, is her crimson mouth,
Her cheeks are as the fading stain
Where the peach reddens to the south.

O twining hands! O delicate
White body made for love and pain!
O House of love! O desolate
Pale flower beaten by the rain!

Chanson [51]

Ring of gold and milk-white dove
Are goodly gifts for thee,
And a hempen rope for your own love
To hang upon a tree.

For you a House of Ivory,
(Roses are white in the rose-bower)!
A narrow bed for me to lie,
(White, O white, is the hemlock flower)!

Myrtle and jessamine for you,
(O the red rose is fair to see)!
For me the cypress and the rue,
(Finest of all is rosemary)!

For you three lovers of your hand,
(Green grass where a man lies dead)!
For me three paces on the sand,
(Plant lilies at my head)!

CHARMIDES

Charmides

I

He was a Grecian lad, who coming home
  With pulpy figs and wine from Sicily
Stood at his galley's prow, and let the foam
  Blow through his crisp brown curls unconsciously,
And holding wave and wind in boy's despite
Peered from his dripping seat across the wet and stormy
    night.

Till with the dawn he saw a burnished spear
  Like a thin thread of gold against the sky,
And hoisted sail, and strained the creaking gear,
  And bade the pilot head her lustily
Against the nor'west gale, and all day long
Held on his way, and marked the rowers' time with
    measured song,

And when the faint Corinthian hills were red
  Dropped anchor in a little sandy bay,
And with fresh boughs of olive crowned his head,
  And brushed from cheek and throat the hoary spray,
And washed his limbs with oil, and from the hold
Brought out his linen tunic and his sandals brazen-soled,

And a rich robe stained with the fishes' juice
  Which of some swarthy trader he had bought
Upon the sunny quay at Syracuse,
  And was with Tyrian broideries inwrought,
And by the questioning merchants made his way
Up through the soft and silver woods, and when the
    labouring day

Had spun its tangled web of crimson cloud,
   Clomb the high hill, and with swift silent feet
Crept to the fane unnoticed by the crowd
   Of busy priests, and from some dark retreat
Watched the young swains his frolic playmates bring
The firstling of their little flock, and the shy shepherd fling

The crackling salt upon the flame, or hang
   His studded crook against the temple wall
To Her who keeps away the ravenous fang
   Of the base wolf from homestead and from stall;
And then the clear-voiced maidens 'gan to sing,
And to the altar each man brought some goodly offering,

A beechen cup brimming with milky foam,
   A fair cloth wrought with cunning imagery
Of hounds in chase, a waxen honey-comb
   Dripping with oozy gold which scarce the bee
Had ceased from building, a black skin of oil
Meet for the wrestlers, a great boar the fierce and
    white-tusked spoil

Stolen from Artemis that jealous maid
   To please Athena, and the dappled hide
Of a tall stag who in some mountain glade
   Had met the shaft; and then the herald cried,
And from the pillared precinct one by one
Went the glad Greeks well pleased that they their simple
   vows had done.

And the old priest put out the waning fires
   Save that one lamp whose restless ruby glowed
For ever in the cell, and the shrill lyres
   Came fainter on the wind, as down the road
In joyous dance these country folk did pass,
And with stout hands the warder closed the gates of
   polished brass.

Long time he lay and hardly dared to breathe,
  And heard the cadenced drip of spilt-out wine,
And the rose-petals falling from the wreath
  As the night breezes wandered through the shrine,
And seemed to be in some entrancèd swoon
Till through the open roof above the full and brimming
    moon

Flooded with sheeny waves the marble floor,
  When from his nook up leapt the venturous lad,
And flinging wide the cedar-carven door
  Beheld an awful image saffron-clad
And armed for battle! the gaunt Griffin glared
From the huge helm, and the long lance of wreck and
    ruin flared

Like a red rod of flame, stony and steeled
  The Gorgon's head its leaden eyeballs rolled,
And writhed its snaky horrors through the shield,
  And gaped aghast with bloodless lips and cold
In passion impotent, while with blind gaze
The blinking owl between the feet hooted in shrill amaze.

The lonely fisher as he trimmed his lamp
  Far out at sea off Sunium, or cast
The net for tunnies, heard a brazen tramp
  Of horses smite the waves, and a wild blast
Divide the folded curtains of the night,
And knelt upon the little poop, and prayed in holy fright.

And guilty lovers in their venery
  Forgat a little while their stolen sweets,
Deeming they heard dread Dian's bitter cry;
  And the grim watchmen on their lofty seats
Ran to their shields in haste precipitate,
Or strained black-bearded throats across the dusky
    parapet.

For round the temple rolled the clang of arms,
   And the twelve Gods leapt up in marble fear,
And the air quaked with dissonant alarums
   Till huge Poseidon shook his mighty spear,
And on the frieze the prancing horses neighed,
And the low tread of hurrying feet rang from the cavalcade.

Ready for death with parted lips he stood,
   And well content at such a price to see
That calm wide brow, that terrible maidenhood,
   The marvel of that pitiless chastity,
Ah! well content indeed, for never wight
Since Troy's young shepherd prince had seen so
    wonderful a sight.

Ready for death he stood, but lo! the air
   Grew silent, and the horses ceased to neigh,
And off his brow he tossed the clustering hair,
   And from his limbs he threw the cloak away;
For whom would not such love make desperate?
And nigher came, and touched her throat, and with hands
    violate

Undid the cuirass, and the crocus gown
   And bared the breasts of polished ivory,
Till from the waist the peplos falling down
   Left visible the secret mystery
Which to no lover will Athena show,
The grand cool flanks, the crescent thighs, the bossy
    hills of snow.

Those who have never known a lover's sin
   Let them not read my ditty, it will be
To their dull ears so musicless and thin
   That they will have no joy of it, but ye
To whose wan cheeks now creeps the lingering smile,
Ye who have learned who Eros is, – O listen yet awhile.

A little space he let his greedy eyes
   Rest on the burnished image, till mere sight
Half swooned for surfeit of such luxuries,
   And then his lips in hungering delight
Fed on her lips, and round the towered neck
He flung his arms, nor cared at all his passion's will to
    check.

Never I ween did lover hold such tryst,
   For all night long he murmured honeyed word,
And saw her sweet unravished limbs, and kissed
   Her pale and argent body undisturbed,
And paddled with the polished throat, and pressed
His hot and beating heart upon her chill and icy breast.

It was as if Numidian javelins
   Pierced through and through his wild and whirling brain,
And his nerves thrilled like throbbing violins
   In exquisite pulsation, and the pain
Was such sweet anguish that he never drew
His lips from hers till overhead the lark of warning flew.

They who have never seen the daylight peer
   Into a darkened room, and drawn the curtain,
And with dull eyes and wearied from some dear
   And worshipped body risen, they for certain
Will never know of what I try to sing,
How long the last kiss was, how fond and late his lingering.

The moon was girdled with a crystal rim,
   The sign which shipmen say is ominous
Of wrath in heaven, the wan stars were dim,
   And the low lightening east was tremulous
With the faint fluttering wings of flying dawn,
Ere from the silent sombre shrine his lover had withdrawn.

Down the steep rock with hurried feet and fast
  Clomb the brave lad, and reached the cave of Pan,
And heard the goat-foot snoring as he passed,
  And leapt upon a grassy knoll and ran
Like a young fawn unto an olive wood
Which in a shady valley by the well-built stood;

And sought a little stream, which well he knew,
  For oftentimes with boyish careless shout
The green and crested grebe he would pursue,
  Or snare in woven net the silver trout,
And down amid the startled reeds he lay
Panting in breathless sweet affright, and waited for the
    day.

On the green bank he lay, and let one hand
  Dip in the cool dark eddies listlessly,
And soon the breath of morning came and fanned
  His hot flushed cheeks, or lifted wantonly
The tangled curls from off his forehead, while
He on the running water gazed with strange and secret smile.

And soon the shepherd in rough woollen cloak;
  With his long crook undid the wattled cotes,
And from the stack a thin blue wreath of smoke
  Curled through the air across the ripening oats,
And on the hill the yellow house-dog bayed
As through the crisp and rustling fern the heavy cattle
    strayed.

And when the light-foot mower went afield
  Across the meadows laced with threaded dew,
And the sheep bleated on the misty weald,
  And from its nest the waking corncrake flew,
Some woodmen saw him lying by the stream
And marvelled much that any lad so beautiful could seem,

Nor deemed him born of mortals, and one said,
  'It is young Hylas, that false runaway
Who with a Naiad now would make his bed
  Forgetting Herakles,' but others, 'Nay,
It is Narcissus, his own paramour,
Those are the fond and crimson lips no woman can allure.'

And when they nearer came a third one cried,
  'It is young Dionysos who has hid
His spear and fawnskin by the river side
  Weary of hunting with the Bassarid,
And wise indeed were we away to fly:
They live not long who on the gods immortal come to spy.'

So turned they back, and feared to look behind,
  And told the timid swain how they had seen
Amid the reeds some woodland God reclined,
  And no man dared to cross the open green,
And on that day no olive-tree was slain,
Nor rushes cut, but all deserted was the fair domain,

Save when the neat-herd's lad, his empty pail
  Well slung upon his back, with leap and bound
Raced on the other side, and stopped to hail,
  Hoping that he some comrade new had found,
And gat no answer, and then half afraid
Passed on his simple way, or down the still and silent
    glade

A little girl ran laughing from the farm,
  Not thinking of love's secret mysteries,
And when she saw the white and gleaming arm
  And all his manlihood, with longing eyes
Whose passion mocked her sweet virginity
Watched him awhile, and then stole back sadly and wearily.

Far off he heard the city's hum and noise,
    And now and then the shriller laughter where
The passionate purity of brown-limbed boys
    Wrestled or raced in the clear healthful air,
And now and then a little tinkling bell
As the shorn wether led the sheep down to the mossy well.

Through the grey willows danced the fretful gnat,
    The grasshopper chirped idly from the tree,
In sleek and oily coat the water-rat
    Breasting the little ripples manfully
Made for the wild-duck's nest, from bough to bough
Hopped the shy finch, and the huge tortoise crept across the
    slough.

On the faint wind floated the silky seeds
    As the bright scythe swept through the waving grass,
The ouzel-cock splashed circles in the reeds
    And flecked with silver whorls the forest's glass,
    And, marking how the rising waters beat
Against the rolling ship, the pilot cried
To the young helmsman at the stern to luff windward side.

But he, the overbold adulterer,
    A dear profaner of great mysteries,
An ardent amorous idolater,
    When he beheld those grand relentless eyes
Laughed loud for joy, and crying out 'I come'
Leapt from the lofty poop into the chill and churning foam.

Then fell from the high heaven one bright star,
    One dancer left the circling galaxy,
And back to Athens on her clattering car
    In all the pride of venged divinity
Pale Pallas [52] swept with shrill and steely clank,
And a few gurgling bubbles rose where her boy lover sank.

And the mast shuddered as the gaunt owl[53] flew
  With mocking hoots after the wrathful Queen,
And the old pilot bade the trembling crew
  Hoist the big sail, and told how he had seen
Close to the stern a dim and giant form,
And like a dipping swallow the stout ship dashed
    through the storm.

And no man dared to speak of Charmides
  Deeming that he some evil thing had wrought,
And when they reached the strait Symplegades
  They beached their galley on the shore, and sought
The toll-gate of the city hastily,
And in the market showed their brown and pictured
    pottery.

II

But some good Triton-god had ruth, and bare
  The boy's drowned body back to Grecian land,
And mermaids combed his dank and dripping hair
  And smoothed his brow, and loosed his clenching hand,
Some brought sweet spices from far Araby,
And others bade the halcyon sing her softest lullaby.

And when he neared his old Athenian home,
  A mighty billow rose up suddenly
Upon whose oily back the clotted foam
  Lay diapered in some strange fantasy,
And clasping him unto its glassy breast
Swept landward, like a white-maned steed upon a venturous
    quest!

Now where Colonos leans unto the sea
  There lies a long and level stretch of lawn;
The rabbit knows it, and the mountain bee
  For it deserts Hymettus, and the Faun
Is not afraid, for never through the day
Comes a cry ruder than the shout of shepherd lads at play.

But often from the thorny labyrinth
    And tangled branches of the circling wood
The stealthy hunter sees young Hyacinth
    Hurling the polished disk, and draws his hood
Over his guilty gaze, and creeps away,
Nor dares to wind his horn, or – else at the first break of
        day

The Dryads come and throw the leathern ball
    Along the reedy shore, and circumvent
Some goat-eared Pan to be their seneschal
    For fear of bold Poseidon's ravishment,
And loose their girdles, with shy timorous eyes,
Lest from the surf his azure arms and purple beard
        should rise.

On this side and on that a rocky cave,
    Hung with the yellow-belled laburnum, stands;
Smooth is the beach, save where some ebbing wave
    Leaves its faint outline etched upon the sands,
As though it feared to be too soon forgot
By the green rush, its playfellow, – and yet, it is a spot

So small, that the inconstant butterfly
    Could steal the hoarded money from each flower
Ere it was noon, and still not satisfy
    Its over-greedy love, – within an hour
A sailor boy, were he but rude enow
To land and pluck a garland for his galley's painted prow,

Would almost leave the little meadow bare,
    For it knows nothing of great pageantry,
Only a few narcissi here and there
    Stand separate in sweet austerity,
Dotting the un-mown grass with silver stars,
And here and there a daffodil waves tiny scimitars.

Hither the billow brought him, and was glad
   Of such dear servitude, and where the land
Was virgin of all waters laid the lad
   Upon the golden margent of the strand,
And like a lingering lover oft returned
To kiss those pallid limbs which once with intense fire
      burned,

Ere the wet seas had quenched that holocaust,
   That self-fed flame, that passionate lustihead,
Ere grisly death with chill and nipping frost
   Had withered up those lilies white and red
Which, while the boy would through the forest range,
Answered each other in a sweet antiphonal counter-change.

And when at dawn the wood-nymphs, hand-in-hand,
   Threaded the bosky dell, their satyr spied
The boy's pale body stretched upon the sand,
   And feared Poseidon's treachery, and cried,
And like bright sunbeams flitting through a glade
Each startled Dryad sought some safe and leafy ambuscade,

Save one white girl, who deemed it would not be
   So dread a thing to feel a sea-god's arms
Crushing her breasts in amorous tyranny,
   And longed to listen to those subtle charms
Insidious lovers weave when they would win
Some fencèd fortress, and stole back again, nor thought
      it sin

To yield her treasure unto one so fair,
   And lay beside him, thirsty with love's drouth,
Called him soft names, played with his tangled hair,
   And with hot lips made havoc of his mouth
Afraid he might not wake, and then afraid
Lest he might wake too soon fled back, and then, fond
      renegade,

Returned to fresh assault, and all day long
   Sat at his side, and laughed at her new toy,
And held his hand, and sang her sweetest song,
   Then frowned to see how froward was the boy
Who would not with her maidenhood entwine,
Nor knew that three days since his eyes had looked on
    Proserpine,

Nor knew what sacrilege his lips had done,
   But said, 'He will awake, I know him well,
He will awake at evening when the sun
   Hangs his red shield on Corinth's citadel;
This sleep is but a cruel treachery
To make me love him more, and in some cavern of the sea

Deeper than ever falls the fisher's line
   Already a huge Triton blows his horn,
And weaves a garland from the crystalline
   And drifting ocean-tendrils to adorn
The emerald pillars of our bridal bed,
For sphered in foaming silver, and with coral-crownèd head,

We two will sit upon a throne of pearl,
   And a blue wave will be our canopy,
And at our feet the water-snakes will curl
   In all their amethystine panoply
Of diamonded mail, and we will mark
The mullets swimming by the mast storm-foundered bark,

Vermilion-finned with eyes of bossy gold
   Like flakes of crimson light, and the great deep
His glassy-portaled chamber will unfold,
   And we will see the painted dolphins sleep
Cradled by murmuring halcyons on the rocks
Where Proteus in quaint suit of green pastures his
    monstrous flocks.

And tremulous opal-hued anemones
   Will wave their purple fringes where we tread
Upon the mirrored floor, and argosies
   Of fishes flecked with tawny scales will thread
The drifting cordage of the shattered wreck,
And honey-coloured amber beads our twining limbs will
    deck.'

But when that baffled Lord of War the Sun
   With gaudy pennon flying passed away
Into his brazen House, and one by one
   The little yellow stars began to stray
Across the field of heaven, ah! then indeed
She feared his lips upon her lips would never care to feed,

And cried, 'Awake, already the pale moon
   Washes the trees with silver, and the wave
Creeps grey and chilly up this sandy dune,
   The croaking frogs are out, and from the cave
The nightjar shrieks, the fluttering bats repass,
And the brown stoat with hollow flanks creeps through the
    dusky grass.

Nay, though thou art a God, be not so coy,
   For in yon stream there is a little reed
That often whispers how a lovely boy
   Lay with her once upon a grassy mead,
Who when his cruel pleasure he had done
Spread wings of rustling gold and soared aloft into the sun.

Be not so coy, the laurel trembles still
   With great Apollo's kisses, and the fir
Whose clustering sisters fringe the seaward hill
   Hath many a tale of that bold ravisher
Whom men call Boreas, and I have seen
The mocking eyes of Hermes through the poplar's silvery
    sheen.

Even the jealous Naiads call me fair,
   And every morn a young and ruddy swain
Woos me with apples and with locks of hair,
   And seeks to soothe my virginal disdain
By all the gifts the gentle wood-nymphs love;
But yesterday he brought to me an iris-plumaged dove

With little crimson feet, which with its store
   Of seven spotted eggs the cruel lad
Had stolen from the lofty sycamore
   At daybreak, when her amorous comrade had
Flown off in search of berried juniper
Which most they love; the fretful wasp, that earliest
    vintager

Of the blue grapes, hath not persistency
   So constant as this simple shepherd-boy
For my poor lips, his joyous purity
   And laughing sunny eyes might well decoy
A Dryad from her oath to Artemis;
For very beautiful is he, his mouth was made to kiss;

His argent forehead, like a rising moon
   Over the dusky hills of meeting brows,
Is crescent shaped, the hot and Tyrian noon
   Leads from the myrtle-grove no goodlier spouse
For Cytheraea, the first silky down
Fringes his blushing cheeks, and his young limbs are
    strong and brown:

And he is rich, and fat and fleecy herds
   Of bleating sheep upon his meadows lie,
And many an earthen bowl of yellow curds
   Is in his homestead for the thievish fly
To swim and drown in, the pink clover mead
Keeps its sweet store for him, and he can pipe on oaten
    reed.

And yet I love him not; it was for thee
   I kept my love; I knew that thou would'st come
To rid me of this pallid chastity,
   Thou fairest flower of the flowerless foam
Of all the wide Aegean, brightest star
Of ocean's azure heavens where the mirrored planets are!

I knew that thou would'st come, for when at first
   The dry wood burgeoned, and the sap of Spring
Swelled in my green and tender bark or burst
   To myriad multitudinous blossoming
Which mocked the midnight with its mimic moons
That did not dread the dawn, and first the thrushes'
   rapturous tunes

Startled the squirrel from its granary,
   And cuckoo flowers fringed the narrow lane,
Through my young leaves a sensuous ecstasy
   Crept like new wine, and every mossy vein
Throbbed with the fitful pulse of amorous blood,
And the wild winds of passion shook my slim stem's
   maidenhood.

The trooping fawns at evening came and laid
   Their cool black noses on my lowest boughs,
And on my topmost branch the blackbird made
   A little nest of grasses for his spouse,
And now and then a twittering wren would light
On a thin twig which hardly bare the weight of such
   delight.

I was the Attic shepherd's trysting place,
   Beneath my shadow Amaryllis lay,
And round my trunk would laughing Daphnis chase
   The timorous girl, till tired out with play
She felt his hot breath stir her tangled hair,
And turned, and looked, and fled no more from such
   delightful snare.

Then come away unto my ambuscade
　　Where clustering woodbine weaves a canopy
For amorous pleasaunce, and the rustling shade
　　Of Paphian myrtles seems to sanctify
The dearest rites of love; there in the cool
And green recesses of its farthest depth there is a pool,

The ouzel's haunt, the wild bee's pasturage,
　　For round its rim great creamy lilies float
Through their flat leaves in verdant anchorage,
　　Each cup a white-sailed olden-laden boat
Steered by a dragon-fly, – be not afraid
To leave this wan and wave-kissed shore, surely the place
　　　　was made

For lovers such as we; the Cyprian Queen,
　　One arm around her boyish paramour,
Strays often there at eve, and I have seen
　　The moon strip off her misty vestiture
For young Endymion's eyes; be not afraid,
The panther feet of Dian never tread that secret glade.

Nay if thou will'st, back to the beating brine,
　　Back to the boisterous billow let us go,
And walk all day beneath the hyaline
　　Huge vault of Neptune's watery portico,
And watch the purple monsters of the deep
Sport in ungainly play, and from his lair keen Xiphias leap.

For if my mistress find me lying here
　　She will not ruth or gentle pity show,
But lay her boar-spear down, and with austere
　　Relentless fingers string the cornel bow,
And draw the feathered notch against her breast,
And loose the arched cord; ay, even now upon the quest

I hear her hurrying feet, – awake, awake,
　　Thou laggard in love's battle! once at least
Let me drink deep of passion's wine, and slake
　　My parchèd being with the nectarous feast

Which even Gods affect! O come, Love, come,
Still we have time to reach the cavern of thine azure home.'

Scarce had she spoken when the shuddering trees
   Shook, and the leaves divided, and the air
Grew conscious of a God, and the grey seas
   Crawled backward, and a long and dismal blare
Blew from some tasselled horn, a sleuth-hound bayed,
And like a flame a barbed reed flew whizzing down the glade.

And where the little towers of her breast
   Just brake into their milky blossoming,
This murderous paramour, this unbidden guest,
   Pierced and struck deep in horrid chambering,
And ploughed a bloody furrow with its dart,
And dug, a long red road, and cleft with wingèd death her
    heart.

Sobbing her life out with a bitter cry
   On the boy's body fell the Dryad maid,
Sobbing for incomplete virginity,
   And raptures unenjoyed, and pleasures dead,
And all the pain of things unsatisfied,
And the bright drops of crimson youth crept down her
    throbbing side.

Ah! pitiful it was to hear her moan,
   And very pitiful to see her die
Ere she had yielded up her sweets, or known
   The joy of passion, that dread mystery
Which not to know is not to live at all,
And yet to know is to be held in death's most deadly thrall.

But as it hapt the Queen of Cythere,
   Who with Adonis all night long had lain
Within some shepherd's hut in Arcady,
   On team of silver doves and gilded wain
Was journeying Paphos-ward, high up afar
From mortal ken between the mountains and the morning
    star,

And when low down she spied the hapless pail;
   And heard the Oread's faint despairing cry,
Whose cadence seemed to play upon the air
   As though it were a viol, hastily
She bade her pigeons fold each straining plume,
And dropt to earth, and reached the strand, and saw their
    dolorous doom.

For as a gardener turning back his head
   To catch the last notes of the linnet, mows
With careless scythe too near some flower bed,
   And cuts the thorny pillar of the rose,
And with the flower's loosened loveliness
Strews the brown mould; or as some shepherd lad in
    wantonness

Driving his little flock along the mead
   Treads down two daffodils, which side by side
Have lured the lady-bird with yellow brede
   And made the gaudy moth forget its pride,
Treads down their brimming golden chalices
Under light feet which were not made for such rude
    ravages;

Or as a schoolboy tired of his book
   Flings himself down upon the reedy grass
And plucks two water-lilies from the brook,
   And for a time forgets the hour glass,
Then wearies of their sweets, and goes his way,
And lets the hot sun kill them, even so these lovers lay.

And Venus cried, 'It is dread Artemis
   Whose bitter hand hath wrought this cruelty,
Or else that mightier maid whose care it is
   To guard her strong and stainless majesty
Upon the hill Athenian, – alas!
That they who loved so well unloved into death's house
    should pass.'

So with soft hands she laid the boy and girl
    In the great golden waggon tenderly,
Her white throat whiter than a moony pearl
    Just threaded with a blue vein's tapestry
Had not yet ceased to throb, and still her breast
Swayed like a wind-stirred lily in ambiguous unrest.

And then each pigeon spread its milky van,
    The bright car soared into the dawning sky,
And like a cloud the aerial caravan
    Passed over the Aegean silently,
Till the faint air was troubled with the song
From the wan mouths that call on bleeding Thammuz
    all night long.

But when the doves had reached their wonted goal
    Where the wide stair of orbèd marble dips
Its snows into the sea, her fluttering soul
    Just shook the trembling petals of her lips
And passed into the void, and Venus knew
That one fair maid the less would walk amid her retinue,

And bade her servants carve a cedar chest
    With all the wonder of this history,
Within whose scented womb their limbs should rest
    Where olive-trees make tender the blue sky
On the low hills of Paphos, and the Faun
Pipes in the noonday, and the nightingale sings on till
    dawn.

Nor failed they to obey her hest, and ere
    The morning bee had stung the daffodil
With tiny fretful spear, or from its lair
    The waking stag had leapt across the rill
And roused the ouzel, or the lizard crept
Athwart the sunny rock, beneath the grass their
    bodies slept.

And when day brake, within that silver shrine
   Fed by the flames of cressets tremulous,
Queen Venus knelt and prayed to Proserpine
   That she whose beauty made Death amorous
Should beg a guerdon from her pallid Lord,
And let Desire pass across dread Charon's icy ford.

III

In melancholy moonless Acheron,
   Far from the goodly earth and joyous day,
Where no spring ever buds, nor ripening sun
   Weighs down the apple trees, nor flowery May
Chequers with chestnut blooms the grassy floor,
Where thrushes never sing, and piping linnets mate no
     more,

There by a dim and dark Lethaean well
   Young Charmides was lying; wearily
He plucked the blossoms from the asphodel,
   And with its little rifled treasury
Strewed the dull waters of the dusky stream,
And watched the white stars founder, and the land was
     like a dream,

When as he gazed into the watery glass
   And through his brown hair's curly tangles scanned
His own wan face, a shadow seemed to pass
   Across the mirror, and a little hand
Stole into his, and warm lips timidly
Brushed his pale cheeks, and breathed their secret forth
     into a sigh.

Then turned he round his weary eyes and saw,
   And ever nigher still their faces came,
And nigher ever did their young mouths draw
   Until they seemed one perfect rose of flame,
And longing arms around her neck he cast,
And felt her throbbing bosom, and his breath came hot and
     fast,

And all his hoarded sweets were hers to kiss,
   And all her maidenhood was his to slay,
And limb to limb in long and rapturous bliss
   Their passion waxed and waned, – O why essay
To pipe again of love, too venturous reed!
Enough, enough that Eros laughed upon that flowerless
    mead.

Too venturous poesy, O why essay
   To pipe again of passion! fold thy wings
O'er daring Icarus and bid thy lay
   Sleep hidden in the lyre's silent strings
Till thou hast found the old Castalian rill,
Or from the Lesbian waters plucked drowned Sappho's
    golden quill!

Enough, enough that he whose life had been
   A fiery pulse of sin, a splendid shame,
Could in the loveless land of Hades glean
   One scorching harvest from those fields of flame
Where passion walks with naked unshod feet
And is not wounded, – ah! enough that once their lips could
    meet

In that wild throb when all existences
   Seemed narrowed to one single ecstasy
Which dies through its own sweetness and the stress
   Of too much pleasure, ere Persephone
Had bade them serve her by the ebon throne
Of the pale God who in the fields of Enna loosed her zone.

FLOWERS OF GOLD

Impressions

I
Les Silhouettes
The sea is flecked with bars of grey,
The dull dead wind is out of tune,
And like a withered leaf the moon
Is blown across the stormy bay.

Etched clear upon the pallid sand
Lies the black boat: a sailor boy
Clambers aboard in careless joy
With laughing face and gleaming hand.

And overhead the curlews cry,
Where through the dusky upland grass
The young brown-throated reapers pass,
Like silhouettes against the sky.

II
La Fuite de la Lune
To outer senses there is peace,
A dreamy peace on either hand
Deep silence in the shadowy land,
Deep silence where the shadows cease.

Save for a cry that echoes shrill
From some lone bird disconsolate;
A corncrake calling to its mate;
The answer from the misty hill.

And suddenly the moon withdraws
Her sickle from the lightening skies,
And to her sombre cavern flies,
Wrapped in a veil of yellow gauze.

The Grave of Keats

Rid of the world's injustice, and his pain,
    He rests at last beneath God's veil of blue:
    Taken from life when life and love were new
The youngest of the martyrs here is lain,
Fair as Sebastian,[54] and as early slain.
    No cypress shades his grave, no funeral yew,
    But gentle violets weeping with the dew
Weave on his bones an ever-blossoming chain.
O proudest heart that broke for misery!
    O sweetest lips since those of Mitylene!
    O poet-painter of our English Land!
Thy name was writ in water – it shall stand:
    And tears like mine[55] will keep thy memory green,
    As Isabella[56] did her Basil-tree.

                                                    ROME

Theocritus[57]
A Villanelle

O singer of Persephone!
    In the dim meadows desolate
Dost thou remember Sicily?

Still through the ivy flits the bee
    Where Amaryllis lies in state;
O Singer of Persephone!

Simaetha calls on Hecate
    And hears the wild dogs at the gate;
Dost thou remember Sicily?

Still by the light and laughing sea
    Poor Polypheme bemoans his fate;
O Singer of Persephone!

And still in boyish rivalry
    Young Daphnis challenges his mate;
Dost thou remember Sicily?

Slim Lacon keeps a goat for thee,
   For thee the jocund shepherds wait;
O Singer of Persephone!
Dost thou remember Sicily?

In the Gold Room
A Harmony

Her ivory hands on the ivory keys
   Strayed in a fitful fantasy,
Like the silver gleam when the poplar trees
   Rustle their pale leaves listlessly,
   Or the drifting foam of a restless sea
When the waves show their teeth in the flying breeze.

Her gold hair fell on the wall of gold
   Like the delicate gossamer tangles spun
On the burnished disk of the marigold,
   Or the sunflower turning to meet the sun
   When the gloom of the dark blue night is done,
And the spear of the lily is aureoled.

And her sweet red lips on these lips of mine
   Burned like the ruby fire set
In the swinging lamp of a crimson shrine,
   Or the bleeding wounds of the pomegranate,
   Or the heart of the lotus drenched and wet
With the spilt-out blood of the rose-red wine.

Ballade de Marguerite
(Normande)

I am weary of lying within the chase
When the knights are meeting in market-place.

Nay, go not thou to the red-roofed town
Lest the hoofs of the war-horse tread thee down.

But I would not go where the Squires ride,
I would only walk by my Lady's side.

Alack! and alack! thou art overbold,
A Forester's son may not eat off gold.

Will she love me the less that my Father is seen
Each Martinmas day in a doublet green?

Perchance she is sewing at tapestrie,
Spindle and loom are not meet for thee.

Ah, if she is working the arras bright
I might ravel the threads by the fire-light.

Perchance she is hunting of the deer,
How could you follow o'er hill and mere?

Ah, if she is riding with the court,
I might run beside her and wind the morte.

Perchance she is kneeling in St Denys,
(On her soul may our Lady have gramercy!)

Ah, if she is praying in lone chapelle,
I might swing the censer and ring the bell.

Come in, my son, for you look sae pale,
The father shall fill thee a stoup of ale.

But who are these knights in bright array?
Is it a pageant the rich folks play?

'Tis the King of England from over sea,
Who has come unto visit our fair countrie.

But why does the curfew toll sae low?
And why do the mourners walk a-row?

O 'tis Hugh of Amiens my sister's son
Who is lying stark, for his day is done.

Nay, nay, for I see white lilies clear,
It is no strong man who lies on the bier.

O 'tis old Dame Jeannette that kept the hall,
I knew she would die at the autumn fall.

Dame Jeannette had not that gold-brown hail,
Old Jeannette was not a maiden fair.

O 'tis none of our kith and none of our kin,
(Her soul may our Lady assoil from sin!)

But I hear the boy's voice chaunting sweet,
'Elle est morte, la Marguerite.'

Come in, my son, and lie on the bed,
And let the dead folk bury their dead.

O mother, you know I loved her true:
O mother, hath one grave room for two?

The Dole of the King's Daughter
(Breton)

Seven stars in the still water,
  And seven in the sky;
Seven sins on the King's daughter,
  Deep in her soul to lie.

Red roses are at her feet,
  (Roses are red in her red-gold hair)
And O where her bosom and girdle meet
  Red roses are hidden there.

Fair is the knight who lieth slain
  Amid the rush and reed,
See the lean fishes that are fain
  Upon dead men to feed.

Sweet is the page that lieth there,
  (Cloth of gold is goodly prey,)
See the black ravens in the air,
  Black, O black as the night are they.

What do they there so stark and dead?
  (There is blood upon her hand)
Why are the lilies flecked with red?
  (There is blood on the river sand.)

There are two that ride from the south and east,
  And two from the north and west,
For the black raven a goodly feast,
  For the King's daughter rest.

There is one man who loves her true,
  (Red, O red, is the stain of gore!)
He hath duggen a grave by the darksome yew,
  (One grave will do for four.)

No moon in the still heaven,
  In the black water none,
The sins on her soul are seven,
  The sin upon his is one.

Amor Intellectualis [58]

Oft have we trod the vales of Castaly
   And heard sweet notes of sylvan music blown
   From antique reeds to common folk unknown:
And often launched our bark upon that sea
Which the nine Muses hold in empery,
   And ploughed free furrows through the wave and foam,
   Nor spread reluctant sail for more safe home
Till we had freighted well our argosy.
Of which despoilèd treasures these remain,
   Sordello's [59] passion, and the honeyed line
Of young Endymion, [60] lordly Tamburlaine [61]
   Driving his pampered jades, and, more than these,
The seven-fold vision of the Florentine, [62]
   And grave-browed Milton's solemn harmonies.

Santa Decca [63]

The Gods are dead: no longer do we bring
   To grey-eyed Pallas crowns of olive-leaves!
   Demeter's child no more hath tithe of sheaves,
And in the noon the careless shepherds sing,
For Pan is dead, and all the wantoning
   By secret glade and devious haunt is o'er:
   Young Hylas seeks the water-springs no more;
Great Pan is dead, and Mary's son is King.

And yet – perchance in this sea-trancèd isle,
   Chewing the bitter fruit of memory,
   Some God lies hidden in the asphodel.
Ah Love! if such there be, then it were well
   For us to fly his anger: nay, but see,
   The leaves are stirring: let us watch awhile.

                                        CORFU

A Vision

Two crownèd Kings, and One that stood alone
    With no green weight of laurels round his head,
    But with sad eyes as one uncomforted,
And wearied with man's never-ceasing moan
For sins no bleating victim can atone,
    And sweet long lips with tears and kisses fed.
    Girt was he in a garment black and red,
And at his feet I marked a broken stone
    Which sent up lilies, dove-like, to his knees.
Now at their sight, my heart being lit with flame,
I cried to Beatricé,[64] 'Who are these?'
And she made answer, knowing well each name,
    'Aeschylos first, the second Sophokles,
    And last (wide stream of tears!) Euripides.'[65]

Impression de Voyage

The sea was sapphire coloured, and the sky
    Burned like a heated opal through the air;
    We hoisted sail; the wind was blowing fair
For the blue lands that to the eastward lie.
From the steep prow I marked with quickening eye
    Zakynthos, every olive grove and creek,
    Ithaca's cliff, Lycaon's snowy peak,
And all the flower-strewn hills of Arcady.
The flapping of the sail against the mast,
    The ripple of the water on the side,
    The ripple of girls' laughter at the stern,
The only sounds: – when 'gan the West to burn,
    And a red sun upon the seas to ride,
    I stood upon the soil of Greece at last!

KATAKOLO

The Grave of Shelley

Like burnt-out torches by a sick man's bed
   Gaunt cypress-trees stand round the sun-bleached stone;
   Here doth the little night-owl make her throne,
And the slight lizard show his jewelled head.
And, where the chaliced poppies flame to red,
   In the still chamber of yon pyramid [66]
   Surely some Old-World Sphinx lurks darkly hid,
Grim warder of this pleasaunce of the dead.

Ah! sweet indeed to rest within the womb
   Of Earth, great mother of eternal sleep,
But sweeter far for thee a restless tomb
   In the blue cavern of an echoing deep,
Or where the tall ships founder in the gloom
   Against the rocks of some wave-shattered steep.

ROME

By the Arno

The oleander on the wall
   Grows crimson in the dawning light,
   Though the grey shadows of the night
Lie yet on Florence like a pall.

The dew is bright upon the hill,
   And bright the blossoms overhead,
   But ah! the grasshoppers have fled,
The little Attic song is still.

Only the leaves are gently stirred
   By the soft breathing of the gale,
   And in the almond-scented vale
The lonely nightingale is heard.

The day will make thee silent soon,
   O nightingale sing on for love!
   While yet upon the shadowy grove
Splinter the arrows of the moon.

Before across the silent lawn
In sea-green vest the morning steals,
And to love's frightened eyes reveals
The long white fingers of the dawn

Fast climbing up the eastern sky
To grasp and slay the shuddering night,
All careless of my heart's delight,
Or if the nightingale should die.

IMPRESSIONS DE THÉÂTRE

Fabien dei Franchi [67]
To my friend Henry Irving

The silent room, the heavy creeping shade,
   The dead that travel fast, the opening door,
   The murdered brother rising through the floor,
The ghost's white fingers on thy shoulders laid,
And then the lonely duel in the glade,
   The broken swords, the stifled scream, the gore,
   Thy grand revengeful eyes when all is o'er, –
These things are well enough, – but thou wert made
   For more august creation! frenzied Lear
   Should at thy bidding wander on the heath
   With the shrill fool to mock him, Romeo
For thee should lure his love, and desperate fear
Pluck Richard's recreant dagger from its sheath –
   Thou trumpet set for Shakespeare's lips to blow!

Phèdre [68]
To Sarah Bernhardt

How vain and dull this common world must seem
   To such a One as thou, who should'st have talked
At Florence with Mirandola, [69] or walked
Through the cool olives of the Academe:
Thou should'st have gathered reeds from a green stream
   For Goat-foot Pan's shrill piping, and have played
   With the white girls in that Phaeacian glade
Where grave Odysseus wakened from his dream.

Ah! surely once some urn of Attic clay
   Held thy wan dust, and thou hast come again
   Back to this common world so dull and vain,
For thou wert weary of the sunless day,
   The heavy fields of scentless asphodel,
   The loveless lips with which men kiss in Hell.

Written at the Lyceum Theatre

I

PORTIA

To Ellen Terry [70]

I marvel not Bassanio was so bold
   To peril all he had upon the lead,
   Or that proud Aragon bent low his head
Or that Morocco's fiery heart grew cold:
For in that gorgeous dress of beaten gold
   Which is more golden than the golden sun
   No woman Veronesé looked upon
Was half so fair as thou whom I behold.
Yet fairer when with wisdom as your shield
   The sober-suited lawyer's gown you donned,
And would not let the laws of Venice yield
   Antonio's heart to that accursèd Jew –
   O Portia! take my heart: it is thy due:
I think I will not quarrel with the Bond.

II

QUEEN HENRIETTA MARIA [71]

To Ellen Terry

In the lone tent,[72] waiting for victory,
   She stands with eyes marred by the mists of pain,
   Like some wan lily overdrenched with rain:
The clamorous clang of arms, the ensanguined sky,
War's ruin, and the wreck of chivalry
   To her proud soul no common fear can bring:
   Bravely she tarrieth for her Lord the King,
Her soul a-flame with passionate ecstasy.
O Hair of Gold! O Crimson Lips! O Face
   Made for the luring and the love of man!
   With thee I do forget the toil and stress,
The loveless road that knows no resting place,
   Time's straitened pulse, the soul's dread weariness,
   My freedom, and my life republican!

Camma [73]

As one who poring on a Grecian urn
   Scans the fair shapes some Attic hand hath made,
   God with slim goddess, goodly man with maid,
And for their beauty's sake is loth to turn
And face the obvious day, must I not yearn
   For many a secret moon of indolent bliss,
   When in the midmost shrine of Artemis
I see thee standing, antique-limbed, and stern?

And yet – methinks I'd rather see thee play
   That serpent of old Nile,[74] whose witchery
Made Emperors drunken, – come, great Egypt, shake
   Our stage with all thy mimic pageants! Nay,
   I am grown sick of unreal passions, make
The world thine Actium, me thine Anthony!

PANTHEA

Panthea

Nay, let us walk from fire unto fire,
  From passionate pain to deadlier delight, –
I am too young to live without desire,
  Too young art thou to waste this summer night
Asking those idle questions which of old
Man sought of seer and oracle, and no reply was told.

For, sweet, to feel is better than to know,
  And wisdom is a childless heritage,
One pulse of passion – youth's first fiery glow, –
  Are worth the hoarded proverbs of the sage:
Vex not thy soul with dead philosophy,
Have we not lips to kiss with, hearts to love and eyes to see!

Dost thou not hear the murmuring nightingale,
  Like water bubbling from a silver jar,
So soft she sings the envious moon is pale,
  That high in heaven she is hung so far
She cannot hear that love-enraptured tune, –
Mark how she wreathes each horn with mist, yon late and
    labouring moon.

White lilies, in whose cups the gold bees dream,
  The fallen snow of petals where the breeze
Scatters the chestnut blossom, or the gleam
  Of boyish limbs in water, – are not these
Enough for thee, dost thou desire more?
Alas! the Gods will give nought else from their eternal store.

For our high Gods have sick and wearied grown
  Of all our endless sins, our vain endeavour
For wasted days of youth to make atone
  By pain or prayer or priest, and never, never,
Hearken they now to either good or ill,
But send their rain upon the just and the unjust at will.

They sit at ease, our Gods they sit at ease,
   Strewing with leaves of rose their scented wine,
They sleep, they sleep, beneath the rocking trees
   Where asphodel and yellow lotus twine,
Mourning the old glad days before they knew
What evil things the heart of man could dream, and
    dreaming do.

And far beneath the brazen floor they see
   Like swarming flies the crowd of little men,
The bustle of small lives, then wearily
   Back to their lotus-haunts they turn again
Kissing each others' mouths, and mix more deep
The poppy-seeded draught which brings soft purple-lidded
    sleep.

There all day long the golden-vestured sun,
   Their torch-bearer, stands with his torch ablaze,
And, when the gaudy web of noon is spun
   By its twelve maidens, through the crimson haze
Fresh from Endymion's arms comes forth the moon,
And the immortal Gods in toils of mortal passions swoon.

There walks Queen Juno through some dewy mead,
   Her grand white feet flecked with the saffron dust
Of wind-stirred lilies, while young Ganymede
   Leaps in the hot and amber-foaming must,
His curls all tossed, as when the eagle bare
The frightened boy from Ida through the blue Ionian air.

There in the green heart of some garden close
   Queen Venus with the shepherd at her side,
Her warm soft body like the briar rose
   Which would be white yet blushes at its pride,
Laughs low for love, till jealous Salmacis
Peers through the myrtle-leaves and sighs for pain of lonely
    bliss.

There never does that dreary north-wind blow
   Which leaves our English forests bleak and bare,

Nor ever falls the swift white-feathered snow,
   Nor ever doth the red-toothed lightning dare
To wake them in the silver-fretted night
When we lie weeping for some sweet sad sin, some dead
      delight.

Alas! they know the far Lethaean spring,
   The violet-hidden waters well they know,
Where one whose feet with tired wandering
   Are faint and broken may take heart and go,
And from those dark depths cool and crystalline
Drink, and draw balm, and sleep for sleepless souls, and
      anodyne.

But we oppress our natures, God or Fate
   Is our enemy, we starve and feed
On vain repentance – O we are born too late!
   What balm for us in bruisèd poppy seed
Who crowd into one finite pulse of time
The joy of infinite love and the fierce pain of infinite crime.

O we are wearied of this sense of guilt,
   Wearied of pleasure's paramour despair,
Wearied of every temple we have built,
   Wearied of every right, unanswered prayer,
For man is weak; God sleeps: and heaven is high:
One fiery-coloured moment: one great love; and lo! we die.

Ah! but no ferry-man with labouring pole
   Nears his black shallop to the flowerless strand,
No little coin of bronze can bring the soul
   Over Death's river to the sunless land,
Victim and wine and vow are all in vain,
The tomb is sealed; the soldiers watch; the dead rise not again.

We are resolved into the supreme air,
   We are made one with what we touch and see,
With our heart's blood each crimson sun is fair,
   With our young lives each spring-impassioned tree
Flames into green, the wildest beasts that range
The moor our kinsmen are, all life is one, and all is change.

With beat of systole and of diastole
    One grand great life[75] throbs through earth's giant heart,
And mighty waves of single Being roll
    From nerveless germ to man, for we are part
Of every rock and bird and beast and hill,
One with the things that prey on us, and one with what we kill.

From lower cells of waking life we pass
    To full perfection; thus the world grows old:
We who are godlike now were once a mass
    Of quivering purple flecked with bars of gold,
Unsentient or of joy or misery,
And tossed in terrible tangles of some wild and wind-swept sea.

This hot hard flame with which our bodies burn
    Will make some meadow blaze with daffodil,
Ay! and those argent breasts of thine will turn
    To water-lilies; the brown fields men till
Will be more fruitful for our love tonight,
Nothing is lost in nature, all things live in Death's despite.

The boy's first kiss, the hyacinth's first bell,
    The man's last passion, and the last red spear
That from the lily leaps, the asphodel
    Which will not let its blossoms blow for fear
Of too much beauty, and the timid shame
Of the young bridegroom at his lover's eyes, – these with the
    same

One sacrament are consecrate, the earth
    Not we alone hath passions hymeneal,
The yellow buttercups that shake for mirth
    At daybreak know a pleasure not less real
Than we do, when in some fresh-blossoming wood,
We draw the spring into our hearts, and feel that life is good.

So when men bury us beneath the yew
    Thy crimson-stained mouth a rose will be,
And thy soft eyes lush bluebells dimmed with dew,
    And when the white narcissus wantonly

Kisses the wind its playmate some faint joy
Will thrill our dust, and we will be again fond maid
   and boy.

And thus without life's conscious torturing pain
   In some sweet flower we will feel the sun,
And from the linnet's throat will sing again,
   And as two gorgeous-mailed snakes will run
Over our graves, or as two tigers creep
Through the hot jungle where the yellow-eyed huge lions sleep

And give them battle! How my heart leaps up
   To think of that grand living after death
In beast and bird and flower, when this cup,
   Being filled too full of spirit, bursts for breath,
And with the pale leaves of some autumn day
The soul earth's earliest conqueror becomes earth's last great
   prey.

O think of it! We shall inform ourselves
   Into all sensuous life, the goat-foot Faun,
The Centaur, or the merry bright-eyed Elves
   That leave their dancing rings to spite the dawn
Upon the meadows, shall not be more near
Than you and I to nature's mysteries, for we shall hear

The thrush's heart beat, and the daisies grow,
   And the wan snowdrop sighing for the sun
On sunless days in winter, we shall know
   By whom the silver gossamer is spun,
Who paints the diapered fritillaries,
On what wide wings from shivering pine to pine the eagle flies.

Ay! had we never loved at all, who knows
   If yonder daffodil had lured the bee
Into its gilded womb, or any rose
   Had hung with crimson lamps its little tree!
Methinks no leaf would ever bud in spring,
But for the lovers' lips that kiss, the poets' lips that sing.

Is the light vanished from our golden sun,
    Or is this daedal-fashioned earth less fair,
That we are nature's heritors, and one
    With every pulse of life that beats the air?
Rather new suns across the sky shall pass,
New splendour[76] come unto the flower, new glory to the grass.

And we two lovers shall not sit afar,
    Critics of nature, but the joyous sea
Shall be our raiment, and the bearded star
    Shoot arrows at our pleasure! We shall be
Part of the mighty universal whole,
And through all aeons mix and mingle with the Kosmic Soul!

We shall be notes in that great Symphony
    Whose cadence circles through the rhythmic spheres,
And all the live World's throbbing heart shall be
    One with our heart; the stealthy creeping years
Have lost their terrors now, we shall not die,
The Universe itself shall be our Immortality.

THE FOURTH MOVEMENT

Impression
Le Réveillon

The sky is laced with fitful red,
　　The circling mists and shadows flee,
　　The dawn is rising from the sea,
Like a white lady from her bed.

　　And jagged brazen arrows fall
　　Athwart the feathers of the night,
　　And a long wave of yellow light
Breaks silently on tower and hall,

　　And spreading wide across the wold
　　Wakes into flight some fluttering bird,
　　And all the chestnut tops are stirred,
And all the branches streaked with gold.

At Verona

How steep the stairs within Kings' houses are
　　For exile-wearied feet[77] as mine to tread,
　　And O how salt and bitter is the bread
Which falls from this Hound's table, – better far
That I had died in the red ways of war;
　　Or that the gate of Florence bare my head,
　　Than to live thus, by all things comraded
Which seek the essence of my soul to mar.

'Curse God and die: what better hope than this?
　　He hath forgotten thee in all the bliss
　　Of his gold city, and eternal day' –
Nay peace: behind my prison's blinded bars
　　I do possess what none can take away
　　My love, and all the glory of the stars.

Apologia

Is it thy will that I should wax and wane,
    Barter my cloth of gold for hodden grey,
And at thy pleasure weave that web of pain
    Whose brightest threads are each a wasted day?

Is it thy will – Love that I love so well –
    That my Soul's House should be a tortured spot
Wherein, like evil paramours, must dwell
    The quenchless flame, the worm that dieth not?

Nay, if it be thy will I shall endure,
    And sell ambition at the common mart,
And let dull failure be my vestiture,
    And sorrow dig its grave within my heart.

Perchance it may be better so – at least
    I have not made my heart a heart of stone,
Nor starved my boyhood of its goodly feast,
    Nor walked where Beauty is a thing unknown.

Many a man hath done so; sought to fence
    In straitened bonds the soul that should be free,
Trodden the dusty road of common sense,
    While all the forest sang of liberty,

Not marking how the spotted hawk in flight
    Passed on wide pinion through the lofty air,
To where some steep untrodden mountain height
    Caught the last tresses of the Sun God's hair.

Or how the little flower he trod upon,
    The daisy, that white-feathered shield of gold,
Followed with wistful eyes the wandering sun
    Content if once its leaves were aureoled.

But surely it is something to have been
　　The best belovèd for a little while,
To have walked hand in hand with Love, and seen
　　His purple wings flit once across thy smile.

Ay! though the gorgèd asp of passion feed
　　On my boy's heart, yet have I burst the bars,
Stood face to face with Beauty, known indeed
　　The Love which moves the Sun and all the stars!

Quia Multum Amavi [78]

Dear Heart, I think the young impassioned priest
   When first he takes from out the hidden shrine
His God imprisoned in the Eucharist,
   And eats the bread, and drinks the dreadful wine,

Feels not such awful wonder as I felt
   When first my smitten eyes beat full on thee,
And all night long before thy feet I knelt
   Till thou wert wearied of Idolatry.

Ah! hadst thou liked me less and loved me more,
   Through all those summer days of joy and rain,
I had not now been sorrow's heritor,
   Or stood a lackey in the House of Pain.

Yet, though remorse, youth's white-faced seneschal,
   Tread on my heels with all his retinue,
I am most glad I loved thee – think of all
   The suns that go to make one speedwell blue!

Silentium Amoris [79]

As often-times the too resplendent sun
   Hurries the pallid and reluctant moon
Back to her sombre cave, ere she hath won
   A single ballad from the nightingale,
   So doth thy Beauty make my lips to fail,
And all my sweetest singing out of tune.

And as at dawn across the level mead
   On wings impetuous some wind will come,
And with its too harsh kisses break the reed
   Which was its only instrument of song,
   So my too stormy passions work me wrong,
And for excess of Love my Love is dumb.

But surely unto Thee mine eyes did show
    Why I am silent, and my lute unstrung;
Else it were better we should part, and go,
    Thou to some lips of sweeter melody,
    And I to nurse the barren memory
Of unkissed kisses, and songs never sung.

Her Voice

The wild bee reels from bough to bough
    With his furry coat and his gauzy wing,
Now in a lily-cup, and now
    Setting a jacinth bell a-swing,
        In his wandering;
Sit closer love: it was here I trow
        I made that vow,

Swore that two lives should be like one
    As long as the sea-gull loved the sea,
As long as the sunflower sought the sun, –
    It shall be, I said, for eternity
        'Twixt you and me!
Dear friend, those times are over and done;
        Love's web is spun.

Look upward where the poplar trees
    Sway and sway in the summer air,
Here in the valley never a breeze
    Scatters the thistledown, but there
        Great winds blow fair
From the mighty murmuring mystical seas,
        And the wave-lashed leas.

Look upward where the white gull screams,
    What does it see that we do not see?
Is that a star? or the lamp that gleams
    On some outward voyaging argosy, –
        Ah! can it be
We have lived our lives in a land of dreams!
        How sad it seems.

Sweet, there is nothing left to say
  But this, that love is never lost,
Keen winter stabs the breasts of May
  Whose crimson roses burst his frost,
    Ships tempest-tossed
Will find a harbour in some bay,
    And so we may.

And there is nothing left to do
  But to kiss once again, and part,
Nay, there is nothing we should rue,
  I have my beauty, – you your Art,
    Nay, do not start,
One world was not enough for two
    Like me and you.

My Voice

Within this restless, hurried, modern world
  We took our hearts' full pleasure – You and I,
And now the white sails of our ship are furled,
  And spent the lading of our argosy.

Wherefore my cheeks before their time are wan
  For very weeping is my gladness fled,
Sorrow has paled my young mouth's vermilion,
  And Ruin draws the curtains of my bed.

But all this crowded life has been to thee
  No more than lyre, or lute, or subtle spell
Of viols, or the music of the sea
  That sleeps, a mimic echo, in the shell.

Taedium Vitae [80]

To stab my youth with desperate knives, to wear
This paltry age's gaudy livery,
To let each base hand filch my treasury,
To mesh my soul within a woman's hair,
And be mere Fortune's lackeyed groom, – I swear
I love it not! these things are less to me
Than the thin foam that frets upon the sea,
Less than the thistledown of summer air
Which hath no seed: better to stand aloof
Far from these slanderous fools who mock my life
Knowing me not, better the lowliest roof
Fit for the meanest hind to sojourn in,
Than to go back to that hoarse cave of strife
Where my white soul first kissed the mouth of sin.

HUMANITAD

Humanitad [81]

It is full winter now: the trees are bare,
   Save where the cattle huddle from the cold
Beneath the pine, for it doth never wear
   The Autumn's gaudy livery whose gold
Her jealous brother pilfers, but is true
To the green doublet; bitter is the wind, as though it blew

From Saturn's cave; a few thin wisps of hay
   Lie on the sharp black hedges, where the wain
Dragged the sweet pillage of a summer's day
   From the low meadows up the narrow lane;
Upon the half-thawed snow the bleating sheep
Press close against the hurdles, and the shivering house-dogs
    creep

From the shut stable to the frozen stream
   And back again disconsolate, and miss
The bawling shepherds and the noisy team;
   And overhead in circling listlessness
The cawing rooks whirl round the frosted stack,
Or crowd the dripping boughs; and in the fen the ice-pools crack

Where the gaunt bittern stalks among the reeds
   And flaps his wings, and stretches back his neck,
And hoots to see the moon; across the meads
   Limps the poor frightened hare, a little speck;
And a stray seamew with its fretful cry
Flits like a sudden drift of snow against the dull grey sky.

Full winter: and the lusty goodman brings
   His load of faggots from the chilly byre,
And stamps his feet upon the hearth, and flings
   The sappy billets on the waning fire,
And laughs to see the sudden lightening scare
His children at their play; and yet, – the Spring is in the air,

Already the slim crocus stirs the snow,
    And soon yon blanchèd fields will bloom again
With nodding cowslips for some lad to mow,
    For with the first warm kisses of the rain
The winter's icy sorrow breaks to tears,
And the brown thrushes mate, and with bright eyes the rabbit
    peers

From the dark warren where the fir-cones lie,
    And treads one snowdrop under foot, and runs
Over the mossy knoll, and blackbirds fly
    Across our path at evening, and the suns
Stay longer with us; ah! how good to see
Grass-girdled Spring in all her joy of laughing greenery

Dance through the hedges till the early rose,
    (That sweet repentance of the thorny briar!)
Burst from its sheathed emerald and disclose
    The little quivering disk of golden fire
Which the bees know so well, for with it come
Pale boy's-love, sops-in-wine, and daffadillies all in bloom.

Then up and down the field the sower goes,
    While close behind the laughing younker scares
With shrilly whoop the black and thievish crows,
    And then the chestnut-tree its glory wears,
And on the grass the creamy blossom falls
In odorous excess, and faint half-whispered madrigals

Steal from the bluebells' nodding carillons
    Each breezy morn, and then white jessamine,
That star of its own heaven, snap-dragons
    With lolling crimson tongues, and eglantine
In dusty velvets clad usurp the bed
And woodland empery, and when the lingering rose hath shed

Red leaf by leaf its folded panoply,
    And pansies closed their purple lidded eyes,
Chrysanthemums from gilded argosy
    Unload their gaudy scentless merchandise,
And violets getting overbold withdraw
From their shy nooks, and scarlet berries dot the leafless haw.

O happy field! and O thrice happy tree!
  Soon will your Queen in daisy-flowered smock
And crown of flower-de-luce trip down the lea,
  Soon will the lazy shepherds drive their flock
Back to the pasture by the pool, and soon
Through the green leaves will float the hum of murmuring
    bees at noon.

Soon will the glade be bright with bellamour,
  The flower which wantons love, and those sweet nuns
Vale-lilies in their snowy vestiture
  Will tell their beaded pearls, and carnations
With mitred dusky leaves will scent the wind,
And straggling traveller's-joy each hedge with yellow stars
    will bind.

Dear Bride of Nature and most bounteous Spring!
  That canst give increase to the sweet-breath'd kine,
And to the kid its little horns, and bring
  The soft and silky blossoms to the vine,
Where is that old nepenthe which of yore
Man got from poppy root and glossy-berried mandragore!

There was a time when any common bird
  Could make me sing in unison, a time
When all the strings of boyish life were stirred
  To quick response or more melodious rhyme
By every forest idyll; – do I change?
Or rather doth some evil thing through thy fair pleasaunce
    range?

Nay, nay, thou art the same: 'tis I who seek
  To vex with sighs thy simple solitude,
And because fruitless tears bedew my cheek
  Would have thee weep with me in brotherhood;
Fool! shall each wronged and restless spirit dare
To taint such wine with the salt poison of his own despair!

Thou art the same: 'tis I whose wretched soul
   Takes discontent to be its paramour,
And gives its kingdom to the rude control
   Of what should be its servitor, – for sure
Wisdom is somewhere, though the stormy sea
Contain it not, and the huge deep answer ' 'Tis not in me.'

To burn with one clear flame,[82] to stand erect
   In natural honour, not to bend the knee
In profitless prostrations whose effect
   Is by itself condemned, what alchemy
Can teach me this? what herb Medea brewed
Will bring the unexultant peace of essence not subdued?

The minor chord which ends the harmony,
   And for its answering brother waits in vain
Sobbing for incompleted melody,
   Dies a Swan's death; but I the heir of pain,
A silent Memnon with blank lidless eyes,
Wait for the light and music of those suns which never rise.

The quenched-out torch, the lonely cypress-gloom,
   The little dust stored in the narrow urn,
The gentle XAIPE[83] of the Attic tomb, –
   Were not these better far than to return
To my old fitful restless malady,
Or spend my days within the voiceless cave of misery?

Nay! for perchance that poppy-crownèd God
   Is like the watcher by a sick man's bed
Who talks of sleep but gives it not; his rod
   Hath lost its virtue, and, when all is said,
Death is too rude, too obvious a key
To solve one single secret in a life's philosophy.

And Love! that noble madness, whose august
   And inextinguishable might can slay
The soul with honeyed drugs, – alas! I must
   From such sweet ruin play the runaway,
Although too constant memory never can
Forget the archèd splendour of those brows Olympian

Which for a little season made my youth
   So soft a swoon of exquisite indolence
That all the chiding of more prudent Truth
   Seemed the thin voice of jealousy, – O Hence
Thou huntress deadlier than Artemis!
Go seek some other quarry! for of thy too perilous bliss

My lips have drunk enough, – no more, no more, –
   Though Love himself should turn his gilded prow
Back to the troubled waters[84] of this shore
   Where I am wrecked and stranded, even now
The chariot wheels of passion sweep too near,
Hence! Hence! I pass unto a life more barren, more austere.

More barren – ay, those arms will never lean
   Down through the trellised vines and draw my soul
In sweet reluctance through the tangled green;
   Some other head must wear that aureole,
For I am Hers who loves not any man
Whose white and stainless bosom bears the sign Gorgonian.[85]

Let Venus go and chuck her dainty page,
   And kiss his mouth, and toss his curly hair,
With net and spear and hunting equipage
   Let young Adonis to his tryst repair,
But me her fond and subtle-fashioned spell
Delights no more, though I could win her dearest citadel.

Ay, though I were that laughing shepherd boy
   Who from Mount Ida saw the little cloud
Pass over Tenedos and lofty Troy
   And knew the coming of the Queen, and bowed
In wonder at her feet, not for the sake
Of a new Helen would I bid her hand the apple take.

Then rise supreme Athena argent-limbed!
   And, if my lips be music-less, inspire
At least my life: was not thy glory hymned
   By One who gave to thee his sword and lyre[86]
Like Aeschylos at well-fought Marathon,
And died to show that Milton's England still could bear a son!

And yet I cannot tread the Portico
   And live without desire, fear and pain,
Or nurture that wise calm which long ago
   The grave Athenian [87] master taught to men,
Self-poised, self-centred, and self-comforted,
To watch the world's vain phantasies go by with un-bowed
    head.

Alas! that serene brow those eloquent lips,
   Those eyes that mirrored all eternity,
Rest in their own Colonos, an eclipse
   Hath come on Wisdom, and Mnemosyne
Is childless; in the night which she had made
For lofty secure flight Athena's owl itself hath strayed.

Nor much with Science do I care to climb,
   Although by strange and subtle witchery
She draw the moon from heaven: the Muse Time
   Unrolls her gorgeous-coloured tapestry
To no less eager eyes; often indeed
In the great epic of Polymnia's [88] scroll I love to read

How Asia sent her myriad hosts to war
   Against a little town, and panoplied
In gilded mail with jewelled scimitar,
   White-shielded, purple-crested, rode the Mede
Between the waving poplars and the sea
Which men call Artemisium, till he saw Thermopylae [89]

Its steep ravine spanned by a narrow wall,
   And on the nearer side a little brood
Of careless lions holding festival!
   And stood amazed at such hardihood,
And pitched his tent upon the reedy shore,
And stayed two days to wonder, and then crept at midnight
    o'er

Some unfrequented height, and coming down
   The autumn-forests treacherously slew
What Sparta held most dear and was the crown

Of far Eurotas, and passed on, nor knew
How God had staked an evil net for him
In the small bay at Salamis, – and yet, the page grows dim,

Its cadenced Greek delights me not, I feel
    With such a goodly time too out of tune
To love it much: for like the Dial's wheel
    That from its blinded darkness strikes the noon
Yet never sees the sun, so do my eyes
Restlessly follow that which from my cheated vision flies.

O for one grand unselfish simple life
    To teach us what is Wisdom! speak ye hills
Of lone Helvellyn,[90] for this note of strife
    Shunned your untroubled crags and crystal rills,
Where is that Spirit which living blamelessly
Yet dared to kiss the smitten mouth of his own century!

Speak ye Rydalian laurels![91] where is He
    Whose gentle head ye sheltered, that pure soul
Whose gracious days of uncrowned majesty
    Through lowliest conduct touched the lofty goal
Where Love and Duty mingle! Him at least
The most high Laws were glad of, He had sat at Wisdom's
        feast,

But we are Learning's changelings, know by rote
    The clarion watchword of each Grecian school
And follow none, the flawless sword which smote
    The pagan Hydra is an effete tool
Which we ourselves have blunted, what man now
Shall scale the august ancient heights and to old Reverence
        bow?

One such indeed I saw, but, Ichabod![92]
    Gone is that last dear son of Italy,[93]
Who being man died for the sake of God,
    And whose un-risen bones sleep peacefully,
O guard him, guard him well, my Giotto's tower,[94]
Thou marble lily of the lily town! Let not the lour

Of the rude tempest vex his slumber, or
   The Arno with its tawny troubled gold
O'er-leap its marge, no mightier conqueror
   Clomb the high Capitol in the days of old
When Rome was indeed Rome, for Liberty
Walked like a Bride beside him, at which sight pale Mystery

Fled shrieking to her farthest sombrest cell
   With an old man who grabbled rusty keys,
Fled shuddering, for that immemorial knell
   With which oblivion buries dynasties
Swept like a wounded eagle on the blast,
As to the holy heart of Rome the great triumvir passed.

He knew the holiest heart and heights of Rome,
   He drave the base wolf from the lion's lair,
And now lies dead by that empyreal dome
   Which overtops Valdarno hung in air
By Brunelleschi – O Melpomene
Breathe through thy melancholy pipe thy sweetest threnody!

Breathe through the tragic stops such melodies
   That Joy's self may grow jealous, and the Nine[95]
Forget awhile their discreet emperies,
   Mourning for him who on Rome's lordliest shrine
Lit for men's lives the light of Marathon,
And bare to sun-forgotten fields the fire of the sun!

O guard him, guard him well, my Giotto's tower,
   Let some young Florentine each eventide
Bring coronals of that enchanted flower
   Which the dim woods of Vallombrosa hide,
And deck the marble tomb wherein he lies
Whose soul is as some mighty orb unseen of mortal eyes.

Some mighty orb whose cycled wanderings,
   Being tempest-driven to the farthest rim
Where Chaos meets Creation and the wings
   Of the eternal chanting Cherubim
Are pavilioned on Nothing, passed away
Into a moonless void, – and yet, though he is dust and clay,

He is not dead, the immemorial Fates
   Forbid it, and the closing shears refrain,
Lift up your heads ye everlasting gates!
   Ye argent clarions, sound a loftier strain!
For the vile thing he hated lurks within
Its sombre house, alone with God and memories of sin.

Still what avails it that she sought her cave
   That murderous mother of red harlotries?
At Munich on the marble architrave [96]
   The Grecian boys die smiling, but the seas
Which wash Aegina fret in loneliness
Not mirroring their beauty, so our lives grow colourless

For lack of our ideals, if one star
   Flame torch-like in the heavens the unjust
Swift daylight kills it, and no trump of war
   Can wake to passionate voice the silent dust
Which was Mazzini once! rich Niobe
For all her stony sorrows hath her sons, but Italy!

What Easter Day shall make her children rise,
   Who were not Gods yet suffered? what sure feet
Shall find their grave-clothes folded? what clear eyes
   Shall see them bodily? O it were meet
To roll the stone from off the sepulchre
And kiss the bleeding roses of their wounds, in love of Her

Our Italy! our mother visible!
   Most blessed among nations and most sad,
For whose dear sake the young Calabrian fell
   That day at Aspromonte [97] and was glad
That in an age when God was bought and sold
One man could die for Liberty! but we, burnt out and cold,

See Honour smitten on the cheek and gyves
   Bind the sweet feet of Mercy: Poverty
Creeps through our sunless lanes and with sharp knives
   Cuts the warm throats of children stealthily,
And no word said: – O we are wretched men
Unworthy of our great inheritance! where is the pen

Of austere Milton? where the mighty sword
   Which slew its master righteously? the years
Have lost their ancient leader, and no word
   Breaks from the voiceless tripod on our ears:
While as a ruined mother in some spasm
Bears a base child and loathes it, so our best enthusiasm

Genders unlawful children, Anarchy
   Freedom's own Judas, the vile prodigal
Licence who steals the gold of Liberty
   And yet has nothing, Ignorance the real
One Fratricide since Cain, Envy the asp
That stings itself to anguish, Avarice whose palsied grasp

Is in its extent stiffened, moneyed Greed
   For whose dull appetite men waste away
Amid the whirr of wheels and are the seed
   Of things which slay their sower, these each day
Sees rife in England, and the gentle feet
Of Beauty tread no more the stones of each unlovely street.

What even Cromwell spared is desecrated
   By weed and worm, left to the stormy play
Of wind and beating snow, or renovated
   By more destructful hands: Time's worst decay
Will wreathe its ruins with some loveliness,
But these new Vandals can but make a rain-proof barrenness.

Where is that Art which bade the Angels sing
   Through Lincoln's lofty choir, till the air
Seems from such marble harmonies to ring
   With sweeter song than common lips can dare
To draw from actual reed? ah! where is now
The cunning hand which made the flowering hawthorn
     branches bow

For Southwell's arch, and carved the House of One
   Who loved the lilies of the field with all
Our dearest English flowers? the same sun
   Rises for us: the seasons natural
Weave the same tapestry of green and grey:
The unchanged hills are with us: but that Spirit hath passed
     away.

And yet perchance it may be better so,
    For Tyranny is an incestuous Queen,
Murder her brother is her bedfellow,
    And the Plague chambers with her: in obscene
And bloody paths her treacherous feet are set;
Better the empty desert and a soul inviolate!

For gentle brotherhood, the harmony
    Of living in the healthful air, the swift
Clean beauty of strong limbs when men are free
    And women chaste, these are the things which lift
Our souls up more than even Agnolo's
Gaunt blinded Sibyl poring o'er the scroll of human woes,

Or Titian's little maiden on the stair
    White as her own sweet lily and as tall,
Or Mona Lisa smiling through her hair, –
    Ah! somehow life is bigger after all
Than any painted Angel, could we see
The God that is within us! The old Greek serenity

Which curbs the passion of that level line
    Of marble youths, who with untroubled eyes
And chastened limbs ride round Athena's shrine
    And mirror her divine economies,
And balanced symmetry of what in man
Would else wage ceaseless warfare, – this at least within the
    span

Between our mother's kisses and the grave
    Might so inform our lives, that we could win
Such mighty empires that from her cave
    Temptation would grow hoarse, and pallid Sin
Would walk ashamed of his adulteries,
And Passion creep from out the House of Lust with startled
    eyes.

To make the Body and the Spirit one [98]
    With all right things, till no thing live in vain
From morn to noon, but in sweet unison

With every pulse of flesh and throb of brain
The Soul in flawless essence high enthroned,
Against all outer vain attack invincibly bastioned,

Mark with serene impartiality
    The strife of things, and yet be comforted,
Knowing that by the chain causality
    All separate existences are wed
Into one supreme whole, whose utterance
Is joy, or holier praise! ah! surely this were governance

Of Life in most august omnipresence,
    Through which the rational intellect would find
In passion its expression, and mere sense,
    Ignoble else, lend fire to the mind,
And being joined with it in harmony
More mystical than that which binds the stars planetary,

Strike from their several tones one octave chord
    Whose cadence being measureless would fly
Through all the circling spheres, then to its Lord
    Return refreshed with its new empery
And more exultant power, – this indeed
Could we but reach it were to find the last, the perfect creed.

Ah! it was easy when the world was young
    To keep one's life free and inviolate,
From our sad lips another song is rung,
    By our own hands our heads are desecrate,
Wanderers in drear exile, and dispossessed
Of what should be our own, we can but feed on wild unrest.

Somehow the grace, the bloom of things has flown,
    And of all men we are most wretched who
Must live each other's lives and not our own
    For very pity's sake and then undo
All that we lived for – it was otherwise
When soul and body seemed to blend in mystic symphonies.

But we have left those gentle haunts to pass
   With weary feet to the new Calvary,
Where we behold, as one who in a glass
   Sees his own face, self-slain Humanity,
And in the dumb reproach of that sad gaze
Learn what an awful phantom the red hand of man can raise.

O smitten mouth! O forehead crowned with thorn!
   O chalice of all common miseries!
Thou for our sakes that loved thee not hast borne
   An agony of endless centuries,
And we were vain and ignorant nor knew
That when we stabbed thy heart it was our own real hearts we
   slew.

Being ourselves the sowers and the seeds,
   The night that covers and the lights that fade,
The spear that pierces and the side that bleeds,
   The lips betraying and the life betrayed;
The deep hath calm: the moon hath rest: but we
Lords of the natural world are yet our own dread enemy.

Is this the end of all that primal force
   Which, in its changes being still the same,
From eyeless Chaos cleft its upward course,
   Through ravenous seas and whirling rocks and flame,
Till the suns met in heaven and began
Their cycles, and the morning stars sang, and the Word was
   Man!

Nay, nay, we are but crucified, and though
   The bloody sweat falls from our brows like rain,
Loosen the nails – we shall come down I know,
   Staunch the red wounds – we shall be whole again,
No need have we of hyssop-laden rod,
That which is purely human, that is Godlike, that is God.

FLOWER OF LOVE

῎μωλ ῎πιλϛοχ Ξϛῶ χ [99]

Sweet, I blame you not, for mine the fault was, had I not been
    made of common clay
I had climbed the higher heights unclimbed yet, seen the fuller air,
    the larger day.

From the wildness of my wasted passion I had struck a better,
    clearer song,
Lit some lighter light of freer freedom, battled with some Hydra-
    headed wrong.

Had my lips been smitten into music by the kisses that but made
    them bleed,
You had walked with Bice and the angels on that verdant and
    enamelled mead.

I had trod the road which Dante treading saw the suns of seven
    circles shine,
Ay! perchance had seen the heavens opening, as they opened to
    the Florentine.

And the mighty nations would have crowned me, who am
    crownless now and without name,
And some orient dawn had found me kneeling on the threshold of
    the House of Fame.

I had sat within that marble circle where the oldest bard is as the
    young,
And the pipe is ever dropping honey, and the lyre's strings are ever
    strung.

Keats had lifted up his hymeneal curls from out the poppy-seeded
    wine,
With ambrosial mouth had kissed my forehead, clasped the hand
    of noble love in mine.

And at springtide, when the apple-blossoms brush the burnished
    bosom of the dove,
Two young lovers lying in an orchard would have read the story of
    our love.

Would have read the legend of my passion, known the bitter secret
    of my heart,
Kissed as we have kissed, but never parted as we two are fated now
    to part.

For the crimson flower of our life is eaten by the cankerworm of
    truth,
And no hand can gather up the fallen withered petals of the rose of
    youth.

Yet I am not sorry that I loved you – ah! what else had I a boy to
    do, –
For the hungry teeth of time devour, and the silent-footed years
    pursue.

Rudderless, we drift athwart a tempest, and when once the storm
    of youth is past,
Without lyre, without lute or chorus, Death the silent pilot comes
    at last.

And within the grave there is no pleasure, for the blindworm
    battens on the root,
And Desire shudders into ashes, and the tree of Passion bears no
    fruit.

Ah! what else had I to do but love you, God's own mother was less
    dear to me,
And less dear the Cytheraean rising like an argent lily from the sea.

I have made my choice, have lived my poems, and, though youth
    is gone in wasted days,
I have found the lover's crown of myrtle better than the poet's
    crown of bays.

UNCOLLECTED POEMS

From Spring Days to Winter
for Music

In the glad springtime when leaves were green,
   O merrily the throstle sings!
I sought, amid the tangled sheen,
Love whom mine eyes had never seen,
   O the glad dove has golden wings!

Between the blossoms red and white,
   O merrily the throstle sings!
My love first came into my sight,
O perfect vision of delight,
   O the glad dove has golden wings!

The yellow apples glowed like fire,
   O merrily the throstle sings!
O Love too great for lip or lyre,
Blown rose of love and of desire,
   O the glad dove has golden wings!

But now with snow the tree is grey,
   Ah, sadly now the throstle sings!
My love is dead: ah! well-a-day,
See at her silent feet I lay
   A dove with broken wings!
   Ah, Love! ah, Love! that thou wert slain –
Fond Dove, fond Dove return again!

°ἵμιξοξ, αἴμιξοξ εἰπ�Ÿ, τὸ δΥ εὖ ξιλ ϕ [100]

O well for him who lives at ease
　　With garnered gold in wide domain,
　　Nor heeds the splashing of the rain,
The crashing down of forest trees.

O well for him who ne'er hath known
　　The travail of the hungry years,
　　A father grey with grief and tears,
A mother weeping all alone.

But well for him whose foot hath trod
　　The weary road of toil and strife,
　　Yet from the sorrows of his life
Builds ladders to be nearer God. [101]

The True Knowledge

　　　… ἀξαηλαέφχ δΥ 'ψει
ϛέοξ νεϛέϊειξ ὥστε λ ϛπινοξ στ ψωξ,
λαὶ τὸξ νὲξ εἶξαι τὸξ δὲ νά [102]

Thou knowest all; [103] I seek in vain
　　What lands to till or sow with seed –
　　The land is black with briar and weed,
Nor cares for falling tears or rain.

Thou knowest all; I sit and wait
　　With blinded eyes and hands that fail,
　　Till the last lifting of the veil
And the first opening of the gate.

Thou knowest all; I cannot see.
　　I trust I shall not live in vain,
　　I know that we shall meet again
In some divine eternity.

Impressions

I
Le Jardin

The lily's withered chalice falls
   Around its rod of dusty gold,
   And from the beech-trees on the wold
The last wood-pigeon coos and calls.

The gaudy leonine sunflower
   Hangs black and barren on its stalk,
   And down the windy garden walk
The dead leaves scatter, – hour by hour.

Pale privet-petals white as milk
   Are blown into a snowy mass:
   The roses lie upon the grass
Like little shreds of crimson silk.

II
La Mer

A white mist drifts across the shrouds,
   A wild moon in this wintry sky
   Gleams like an angry lion's eye
Out of a mane of tawny clouds.

The muffled steersman at the wheel
   Is but a shadow in the gloom; –
   And in the throbbing engine-room
Leap the long rods of polished steel.

The shattered storm has left its trace
   Upon this huge and heaving dome,
   For the thin threads of yellow foam
Float on the waves like ravelled lace.

Under the Balcony

O beautiful star with the crimson mouth!
  O moon with the brows of gold!
Rise up, rise up, from the odorous south!
    And light for my love her way,
    Lest her little feet should stray
  On the windy hill and the wold!
O beautiful star with the crimson mouth!
  O moon with the brows of gold!

O ship that shakes on the desolate sea:
  O ship with the wet, white sail!
Put in, put in, to the port to me!
    For my love and I would go
    To the land where the daffodils blow
  In the heart of a violet dale!
O ship that shakes on the desolate sea!
  O ship with the wet, white sail!

O rapturous bird with the low, sweet note!
  O bird that sits on the spray!
Sing on, sing on, from your soft brown throat!
    And my love in her little bed
    Will listen, and lift her head
  From the pillow, and come my way!
O rapturous bird with the low, sweet note!
  O bird that sits on the spray!

O blossom that hangs in the tremulous air!
  O blossom with lips of snow!
Come down, come down, for my love to wear!
    You will die on her head in a crown,
    You will die in a fold of her gown,
  To her little light heart you will go!
O blossom that hangs in the tremulous air!
  O blossom with lips of snow!

The Harlot's House

We caught the tread of dancing feet,
We loitered down the moonlit street,
And stopped beneath the harlot's house.

Inside, above the din and fray,
We heard the loud musicians play
The 'Treues Liebes Herz' of Strauss.

Like strange mechanical grotesques,
Making fantastic arabesques,
The shadows raced across the blind.

We watched the ghostly dancers spin
To sound of horn and violin,
Like black leaves wheeling in the wind.

Like wire-pulled automatons,
Slim silhouetted skeletons
Went sidling through the slow quadrille.

They took each other by the hand,
And danced a stately saraband;
Their laughter echoed thin and shrill.

Sometimes a clockwork puppet pressed
A phantom lover to her breast,
Sometimes they seemed to try to sing.

Sometimes a horrible marionette
Came out, and smoked its cigarette
Upon the steps like a live thing.

Then, turning to my love, I said,
'The dead are dancing with the dead,
The dust is whirling with the dust.'

But she – she heard the violin,
And left my side, and entered in:
Love passed into the house of lust.

Then suddenly the tune went false,
The dancers wearied of the waltz,
The shadows ceased to wheel and whirl.

And down the long and silent street,
The dawn, with silver-sandalled feet,
Crept like a frightened girl.

Le Jardin des Tuileries

This winter air is keen and cold,
    And keen and cold this winter sun,
    But round my chair the children run
Like little things of dancing gold.

Sometimes about the painted kiosk
    The mimic soldiers strut and stride,
    Sometimes the blue-eyed brigands hide
In the bleak tangles of the bosk.

And sometimes, while the old nurse cons
    Her book, they steal across the square,
    And launch their paper navies where
Huge Triton writhes in greenish bronze.

And now in mimic flight they flee,
    And now they rush, a boisterous band –
    And, tiny hand on tiny hand,
Climb up the black and leafless tree.

Ah! cruel tree! if I were you,
    And children climbed me, for their sake
    Though it be winter I would break
Into spring blossoms white and blue!

On the Sale by Auction of Keats's Love Letters

These are the letters which Endymion[104] wrote
    To one he loved in secret, and apart.
    And now the brawlers of the auction mart
Bargain and bid for each poor blotted note,
Ay! for each separate pulse of passion quote
    The merchant's price. I think they love not art
    Who break the crystal of a poet's heart
That small and sickly eyes may glare and gloat.

Is it not said that many years ago,
    In a far Eastern town,[105] some soldiers ran
    With torches through the midnight, and began
To wrangle for mean raiment, and to throw
    Dice for the garments of a wretched man,
Not knowing the God's wonder, or His woe?

The New Remorse

The sin was mine; I did not understand.
    So new is music prisoned in her cave,
    Save where some ebbing desultory wave
Frets with its restless whirls this meagre strand.
And in the withered hollow of this land
    Hath Summer dug herself so deep a grave,
    That hardly can the leaden willow crave
One silver blossom from keen Winter's hand.

But who is this who cometh by the shore?
(Nay, love, look up and wonder!) Who is this
    Who cometh in dyed garments from South?
It is thy new-found Lord, and he shall kiss
    The yet unravished roses of thy mouth,
And I shall weep and worship, as before.

Fantasies Décoratives

I

Le Panneau [106]

Under the rose-tree's dancing shade
   There stands a little ivory girl
   Pulling the leaves of pink and pearl
With pale green nails of polished jade.

The red leaves fall upon the mould,
   The white leaves flutter, one by one,
   Down to a blue bowl where the sun,
Like a great dragon, writhes in gold.

The white leaves float upon the air,
   The red leaves flutter idly down,
   Some fall upon her yellow gown,
And some upon her raven hair.

She takes an amber lute and sings,
   And as she sings a silver crane
   Begins his scarlet neck to strain,
And flap his burnished metal wings.

She takes a lute of amber bright,
   And from the thicket where he lies
   Her lover, with his almond eyes,
Watches her movements in delight.

And now she gives a cry of fear,
   And tiny tears begin to start:
   A thorn has wounded with its dart
The pink-veined sea-shell of her ear.

And now she laughs a merry note:
   There has fallen a petal of the rose
   Just where the yellow satin shows
The blue-veined flower of her throat.

With pale green nails of polished jade,
   Pulling the leaves of pink and pearl,
   There stands a little ivory girl
Under the rose-tree's dancing shade.

II
Les Ballons

Against these turbid turquoise skies
   The light and luminous balloons
   Dip and drift like satin moons,
Drift like silken butterflies;

Reel with every windy gust,
   Rise and reel like dancing girls,
   Float like strange transparent pearls,
Fall and float like silver dust.

Now to the low leaves they cling,
   Each with coy fantastic pose,
   Each a petal of a rose
Straining at a gossamer string.

Then to the tall trees they climb,
   Like thin globes of amethyst,
   Wandering opals keeping tryst
With the rubies of the lime.

Canzonet

   I have no store
  Of gryphon-guarded gold;
    Now, as before,
  Bare is the shepherd's fold.
    Rubies nor pearls
  Have I to gem thy throat;
    Yet woodland girls
  Have loved the shepherd's note.

Then pluck a reed
And bid me sing to thee,
For I would feed
Thine ears with melody,
Who art more fair
Than fairest fleur-de-lys,
More sweet and rare
Than sweetest ambergris.

What dost thou fear?
Young Hyacinth is slain,
Pan is not here,
And will not come again.
No hornèd Faun
Treads down the yellow leas,
No God at dawn
Steals through the olive trees.

Hylas is dead,
Nor will he e'er divine
Those little red
Rose-petalled lips of thine.
On the high hill
No ivory dryads play,
Silver and still
Sinks the sad autumn day.

Symphony in Yellow

An omnibus across the bridge
   Crawls like a yellow butterfly,
   And, here and there, a passer-by
Shows like a little restless midge.

Big barges full of yellow hay
   Are moved against the shadowy wharf,
   And, like a yellow silken scarf,
The thick fog hangs along the quay.

The yellow leaves begin to fade
   And flutter from the Temple elms,
   And at my feet the pale green Thames
Lies like a rod of rippled jade.

In the Forest

Out of the mid-wood's twilight
   Into the meadow's dawn,
Ivory limbed and brown-eyed,
   Flashes my Faun!

He skips through the copses singing,
   And his shadow dances along,
And I know not which I should follow,
   Shadow or song!

O Hunter, snare me his shadow!
   O Nightingale, catch me his strain!
Else moonstruck with music and madness
   I track him in vain!

To My Wife
With a copy of my poems

I can write no stately proem
   As a prelude to my lay;
From a poet to a poem
   I would dare to say.

For if of these fallen petals
   One to you seem fair,
Love will waft it till it settles
   On your hair.

And when wind and winter harden
   All the loveless land,
It will whisper of the garden,
   You will understand.

With a Copy of 'A House of Pomegranates'[107]

Go little book,
To him who, on a lute with horns of pearl,
Sang of the white feet of the Golden Girl:
And bid him look
Into thy pages: it may hap that he
May find that golden maidens dance through thee.

To L. L.[108]

Could we dig up this long-buried treasure,
   Were it worth the pleasure,
We never could learn love's song,
   We are parted too long.

Could the passionate past that is fled
   Call back its dead,
Could we live it all over again,
   Were it worth the pain!

I remember we used to meet
   By an ivied seat,
And you warbled each pretty word
   With the air of a bird;

And your voice had a quaver in it,
   Just like a linnet,
And shook, as the blackbird's throat
   With its last big note;

And your eyes, they were green and grey
   Like an April day,
But lit into amethyst
   When I stooped and kissed;

And your mouth, it would never smile
   For a long, long while
Then it rippled all over with laughter
   Five minutes after.

You were always afraid of a shower,
   Just like a flower:
I remember you started and ran
   When the rain began.

I remember I never could catch you,
   For no one could match you,
You had wonderful, luminous, fleet,
   Little wings to your feet.

I remember your hair – did I tie it?
   For it always ran riot –
Like a tangled sunbeam of gold:
   These things are old.

I remember so well the room,
   And the lilac bloom
That beat at the dripping pane
   In the warm June rain;

And the colour of your gown,
    It was amber-brown,
And two yellow satin bows
    From your shoulders rose.

And the handkerchief of French lace
    Which you held to your face –
Had a small tear left a stain?
    Or was it the rain?

On your hand as it waved adieu
    There were veins of blue;
In your voice as it said good-bye
    Was a petulant cry,

'You have only wasted your life.'
    (Ah, that was the knife!)
When I rushed through the garden gate
    It was all too late.

Could we live it over again,
    Were it worth the pain,
Could the passionate past that is fled
    Call back its dead!

Well, if my heart must break,
    Dear love, for your sake,
It will break in music, I know,
    Poets' hearts break so.

But strange that I was not told
    That the brain can hold
In a tiny ivory cell
    God's heaven and hell.

Désespoir

The seasons send their ruin as they go,
For in the spring the narciss shows its head
Nor withers till the rose has flamed to red,
And in the autumn purple violets blow,
And the slim crocus stirs the winter snow;
Wherefore yon leafless trees will bloom again
And this grey land grow green with summer rain
And send up cowslips for some boy to mow.

But what of life whose bitter hungry sea
Flows at our heels, and gloom of sunless night
Covers the days which never more return?
Ambition, love and all the thoughts that burn
We lose too soon, and only find delight
In withered husks of some dead memory.

Pan

Double Villanelle

I

O goat-foot God of Arcady!
This modern world is grey and old,
And what remains to us of thee?

No more the shepherd lads in glee
Throw apples at thy wattled fold,
O goat-foot God of Arcady!

Nor through the laurels can one see
Thy soft brown limbs, thy beard of gold,
And what remains to us of thee?

And dull and dead our Thames would be,
For here the winds are chill and cold,
O goat-foot God of Arcady!

Then keep the tomb of Helice,
Thine olive-woods, thy vine-clad wold,
And what remains to us of thee?

Though many an unsung elegy
Sleeps in the reeds our rivers hold,
O goat-foot God of Arcady!
Ah, what remains to us of thee?

II

Ah, leave the hills of Arcady,
Thy satyrs and their wanton play,
This modern world hath need of thee.

No nymph or Faun indeed have we,
For Faun and nymph are old and grey,
Ah, leave the hills of Arcady!

This is the land where liberty
Lit grave-browed Milton on his way,
This modern world hath need of thee!

A land of ancient chivalry
Where gentle Sidney saw the day,
Ah, leave the hills of Arcady.

This fierce sea-lion of the sea,
This England lacks some stronger lay,
This modern world hath need of thee!

Then blow some trumpet loud and free,
And give thine oaten pipe away,
Ah, leave the hills of Arcady!
This modern world hath need of thee!

THE SPHINX

to Marcel Schwob in friendship and in admiration

The Sphinx

In a dim corner of my room for longer than my fancy thinks
A beautiful and silent Sphinx has watched me through the shifting
   gloom.

Inviolate and immobile she does not rise she does not stir
For silver moons are naught to her and naught to her the suns that
   reel.

Red follows grey across the air the waves of moonlight ebb and flow
But with the Dawn she does not go and in the night-time she is there.

Dawn follows Dawn and Nights grow old and all the while this
   curious cat
Lies couching on the Chinese mat with eyes of satin rimmed with
   gold.

Upon the mat she lies and leers and on the tawny throat of her
Flutters the soft and silky fur or ripples to her pointed ears.

Come forth, my lovely seneschal! so somnolent, so statuesque!
Come forth you exquisite grotesque! half woman and half animal!

Come forth my lovely languorous Sphinx! and put your head upon my
   knee!
And let me stroke your throat and see your body spotted like the Lynx!

And let me touch those curving claws of yellow ivory and grasp
The tail that like a monstrous Asp coils round your heavy velvet paws!

*

A thousand weary centuries are thine while I have hardly seen
Some twenty summers cast their green for Autumn's gaudy liveries.

But you can read the Hieroglyphs on the great sandstone obelisks,
And you have talked with Basilisks, and you have looked on
     Hippogriffs.

O tell me, were you standing by when Isis to Osiris knelt?
And did you watch the Egyptian melt her union for Antony

And drink the jewel-drunken wine and bend her head in mimic awe
To see the huge proconsul draw the salted tunny from the brine?

And did you mark the Cyprian kiss white Adon on his catafalque?
And did you follow Amenalk, the God of Heliopolis?

And did you talk with Thoth, and did you hear the moon-horned Io
     weep?
And know the painted kings who sleep beneath the wedge-shaped
     Pyramid?

*

Lift up your large black satin eyes which are like cushions where one
     sinks!
Fawn at my feet, fantastic Sphinx! and sing me all your memories!

Sing to me of the Jewish maid who wandered with the Holy Child,
And how you led them through the wild, and how they slept beneath
     your shade.

Sing to me of that odorous green eve when crouching by the marge
You heard from Adrian's gilded barge the laughter of Antinous

And lapped the stream and fed your drouth and watched with hot and
     hungry stare
The ivory body of that rare young slave with his pomegranate mouth!

Sing to me of the Labyrinth in which the twi-formed bull was stalled!
Sing to me of the night you crawled across the temple's granite plinth

When through the purple corridors the screaming scarlet Ibis flew
In terror, and a horrid dew dripped from the moaning Mandragores,

And the great torpid crocodile within the tank shed slimy tears,
And tare the jewels from his ears and staggered back into the Nile,

And the priests cursed you with shrill psalms as in your claws you
    seized their snake
And crept away with it to slake your passion by the shuddering palms.

*

Who were your lovers? who were they who wrestled for you in the
    dust?
Which was the vessel of your Lust? What Leman had you, every day?

Did giant Lizards come and crouch before you on the reedy banks?
Did Gryphons with great metal flanks leap on you in your trampled
    couch?

Did monstrous hippopotami come sidling toward you in the mist?
Did gilt-scaled dragons writhe and twist with passion as you passed
    them by?

And from the brick-built Lycian tomb what horrible Chimera came
With fearful heads and fearful flame to breed new wonders from your
    womb?

*

Or had you shameful secret quests and did you harry to your home
Some Nereid coiled in amber foam with curious rock crystal breasts?

Or did you treading through the froth call to the brown Sidonian
For tidings of Leviathan, Leviathan or Behemoth?

Or did you when the sun was set climb up the cactus-covered slope
To meet your swarthy Ethiop whose body was of polished jet?

Or did you while the earthen skiffs dropped down the grey Nilotic flats
At twilight and the flickering bats flew round the temple's triple glyphs

Steal to the border of the bar and swim across the silent lake
And slink into the vault and make the Pyramid your lúpanar

Till from each black sarcophagus rose up the painted swathèd dead?
Or did you lure unto your bed the ivory-horned Tragelaphos?

Or did you love the god of flies who plagued the Hebrews and was
     splashed
With wine unto the waist? or Pasht, who had green beryls for her eyes?

Or that young god, the Tyrian, who was more amorous than the dove
Of Ashtaroth? or did you love the god of the Assyrian

Whose wings like strange transparent talc, rose high above his hawk-
     faced head,
Painted with silver and with red and ribbed with rods of Oreichalch?

Or did huge Apis from his car leap down and lay before your feet
Big blossoms of the honey-sweet and honey-coloured nenuphar?

*

How subtle-secret is your smile! Did you love none then? Nay I know
Great Ammon was your bedfellow! He lay with you beside the Nile!

The river-horses in the slime trumpeted when they saw him come
Odorous with Syrian galbanum and smeared with spikenard and with
     thyme.

He came along the river bank like some tall galley argent-sailed,
He strode across the waters, mailed in beauty, and the waters sank.

He strode across the desert sand: he reached the valley where you lay:
He waited till the dawn of day: then touched your black breasts with
     his hand.

You kissed his mouth with mouths of flame: you made the hornèd god
     your own:
You stood behind him on his throne: you called him by his secret
     name.

You whispered monstrous oracles into the caverns of his ears:
With blood of goats and blood of steers you taught him monstrous
    miracles.

White Ammon was your bedfellow! Your chamber was the steaming
    Nile!
And with your curved archaic smile you watched his passion come
    and go.

*

With Syrian oils his brows were bright: and wide-spread as a tent at
    noon
His marble limbs made pale the moon and lent the day a larger light.

His long hair was nine cubits' span and coloured like that yellow gem
Which hidden in their garment's hem the merchants bring from
    Kurdistan.

His face was as the must that lies upon a vat of new-made wine:
The seas could not insapphirine the perfect azure of his eyes.

His thick soft throat was white as milk and threaded with thin veins of
    blue:
And curious pearls like frozen dew were broidered on his flowing silk.

*

On pearl and porphyry pedestalled he was too bright to look upon:
For on his ivory breast there shone the wondrous ocean-emerald,

That mystic moonlit jewel which some diver of the Colchian caves
Had found beneath the blackening waves and carried to the Colchian
    witch.

Before his gilded galiot ran naked vine-wreathed corybants,
And lines of swaying elephants knelt down to draw his chariot,

And lines of swarthy Nubians bare up his litter as he rode
Down the great granite-paven road between the nodding peacock-fans.

The merchants brought him steatite from Sidon in their painted ships:
The meanest cup that touched his lips was fashioned from a
    chrysolite.

The merchants brought him cedar chests of rich apparel bound with
    cords:
His train was borne by Memphian lords: young kings were glad to be
    his guests.

Ten hundred shaven priests did bow to Ammon's altar day and night,
Ten hundred lamps did wave their light through Ammon's carven
    house – and now

Foul snake and speckled adder with their young ones crawl from stone
    to stone
For ruined is the house and prone the great rose-marble monolith!

Wild ass or trotting jackal comes and couches in the mouldering gates:
Wild satyrs call unto their mates across the fallen fluted drums.

And on the summit of the pile the blue-faced ape of Horus sits
And gibbers while the fig-tree splits the pillars of the peristyle

*

The god is scattered here and there: deep hidden in the windy sand
I saw his giant granite hand still clenched in impotent despair.

And many a wandering caravan of stately negroes silken-shawled,
Crossing the desert, halts appalled before the neck that none can span.

And many a bearded Bedouin draws back his yellow-striped burnous
To gaze upon the Titan thews of him who was thy paladin.

*

Go, seek his fragments on the moor and wash them in the evening
    dew,
And from their pieces make anew thy mutilated paramour!

Go, seek them where they lie alone and from their broken pieces make
Thy bruisèd bedfellow! And wake mad passions in the senseless stone!

Charm his dull ear with Syrian hymns! he loved your body! oh, be
    kind,
Pour spikenard on his hair, and wind soft rolls of linen round his
    limbs!

Wind round his head the figured coins! stain with red fruits those
    pallid lips!
Weave purple for his shrunken hips! and purple for his barren loins!

*

Away to Egypt! Have no fear. Only one God has ever died.
Only one God has let His side be wounded by a soldier's spear.

But these, thy lovers, are not dead. Still by the hundred-cubit gate
Dog-faced Anubis sits in state with lotus-lilies for thy head.

Still from his chair of porphyry gaunt Memnon strains his lidless eyes
Across the empty land, and cries each yellow morning unto thee.

And Nilus with his broken horn lies in his black and oozy bed
And till thy coming will not spread his waters on the withering corn.

Your lovers are not dead, I know. They will rise up and hear your voice
And clash their cymbals and rejoice and run to kiss your mouth! And
    so,

Set wings upon your argosies! Set horses to your ebon car!
Back to your Nile! Or if you are grown sick of dead divinities

Follow some roving lion's spoor across the copper-coloured plain,
Reach out and hale him by the mane and bid him be your paramour!

Couch by his side upon the grass and set your white teeth in his throat
And when you hear his dying note lash your long flanks of polished
    brass

And take a tiger for your mate, whose amber sides are flecked with
    black,
And ride upon his gilded back in triumph through the Theban gate,

And toy with him in amorous jests, and when he turns, and snarls,
    and gnaws,
O smite him with your jasper claws! and bruise him with your agate
    breasts!

*

Why are you tarrying? Get hence! I weary of your sullen ways,
I weary of your steadfast gaze, your somnolent magnificence.

Your horrible and heavy breath makes the light flicker in the lamp,
And on my brow I feel the damp and dreadful dews of night and
    death.

Your eyes are like fantastic moons that shiver in some stagnant lake,
Your tongue is like a scarlet snake that dances to fantastic tunes,

Your pulse makes poisonous melodies, and your black throat is like
    the hole
Left by some torch or burning coal on Saracenic tapestries.

Away! The sulphur-coloured stars are hurrying through the Western
    gate!
Away! Or it may be too late to climb their silent silver cars!

See, the dawn shivers round the grey gilt-dialled towers, and the rain
Streams down each diamonded pane and blurs with tears the wannish
    day.

What snake-tressed fury fresh from Hell, with uncouth gestures and
    unclean,
Stole from the poppy-drowsy queen and led you to a student's cell?

*

What songless tongueless ghost of sin crept through the curtains of
    the night,
And saw my taper burning bright, and knocked, and bade you enter
    in.

Are there not others more accursed, whiter with leprosies than I?
Are Abana and Pharphar dry that you come here to slake your thirst?

Get hence, you loathsome mystery! Hideous animal, get hence!
You wake in me each bestial sense, you make me what I would not be.

You make my creed a barren sham, you wake foul dreams of sensual
    life,
And Atys with his blood-stained knife were better than the thing I am.

False Sphinx! False Sphinx! By reedy Styx old Charon, leaning on his
    oar,
Waits for my coin. Go thou before, and leave me to my crucifix,

Whose pallid burden, sick with pain, watches the world with wearied
    eyes,
And weeps for every soul that dies, and weeps for every soul in vain.

THE BALLAD OF READING GAOL

In memoriam C. T. W.
sometime trooper of the Royal Horse Guards.
obiit H. M. Prison, Reading, Berkshire, July 7 1896

The Ballad of Reading Gaol

I

He did not wear his scarlet coat,
    For blood and wine are red,
And blood and wine were on his hands
    When they found him with the dead,
The poor dead woman whom he loved,
    And murdered in her bed.

He walked amongst the Trial Men
    In a suit of shabby gray;
A cricket cap was on his head,
    And his step seemed light and gay;
But I never saw a man who looked
    So wistfully at the day.

I never saw a man who looked
    With such a wistful eye
Upon that little tent of blue
    Which prisoners call the sky,
And at every drifting cloud that went
    With sails of silver by.

I walked with other souls in pain,
    Within another ring,
And was wondering if the man had done
    A great or little thing,
When a voice behind me whispered low,
    'That fellow's got to swing.'

Dear Christ! the very prison walls
　　Suddenly seemed to reel,
And the sky above my head became
　　Like a casque of scorching steel;
And, though I was a soul in pain,
　　My pain I could not feel.

I only knew what hunted thought
　　Quickened his step, and why
He looked upon the garish day
　　With such a wistful eye;
The man had killed the thing he loved,
　　And so he had to die.

*

Yet each man kills the thing he loves,
　　By each let this be heard,
Some do it with a bitter look,
　　Some with a flattering word,
The coward does it with a kiss,
　　The brave man with a sword!

Some kill their love when they are young,
　　And some when they are old;
Some strangle with the hands of Lust,
　　Some with the hands of Gold:
The kindest use a knife, because
　　The dead so soon grow cold.

Some love too little, some too long,
　　Some sell, and others buy;
Some do the deed with many tears,
　　And some without a sigh:
For each man kills the thing he loves,
　　Yet each man does not die.

He does not die a death of shame
　　On a day of dark disgrace,
Nor have a noose about his neck,
　　Nor a cloth upon his face,
Nor drop feet foremost through the floor
　　Into an empty space.

*

He does not sit with silent men
  Who watch him night and day;
Who watch him when he tries to weep,
  And when he tries to pray;
Who watch him lest himself should rob
  The prison of its prey.

He does not wake at dawn to see
  Dread figures throng his room,
The shivering Chaplain robed in white,
  The Sheriff stern with gloom,
And the Governor all in shiny black,
  With the yellow face of Doom.

He does not rise in piteous haste
  To put on convict-clothes,
While some coarse-mouthed Doctor gloats, and notes
  Each new and nerve-twitched pose,
Fingering a watch whose little ticks
  Are like horrible hammer-blows.

He does not know that sickening thirst
  That sands one's throat, before
The hangman with his gardener's gloves
  Slips through the padded door,
And binds one with three leathern thongs,
  That the throat may thirst no more.

He does not bend his head to hear
  The Burial Office read,
Nor, while the terror of his soul
  Tells him he is not dead,
Cross his own coffin, as he moves
  Into the hideous shed.

He does not stare upon the air
  Through a little roof of glass:
He does not pray with lips of clay
  For his agony to pass;
Nor feel upon his shuddering cheek
  The kiss of Caiaphas.

II

Six weeks our guardsman walked the yard,
    In the suit of shabby grey:
His cricket cap was on his head,
    And his step seemed light and gay,
But I never saw a man who looked
    So wistfully at the day.

I never saw a man who looked
    With such a wistful eye
Upon that little tent of blue
    Which prisoners call the sky,
And at every wandering cloud that trailed
    Its ravelled fleeces by.

He did not wring his hands, as do
    Those witless men who dare
To try to rear the changeling Hope
    In the cave of black Despair:
He only looked upon the sun,
    And drank the morning air.

He did not wring his hands nor weep,
    Nor did he peek or pine,
But he drank the air as though it held
    Some healthful anodyne;
With open mouth he drank the sun
    As though it had been wine!

And I and all the souls in pain,
    Who tramped the other ring,
Forgot if we ourselves had done
    A great or little thing,
And watched with gaze of dull amaze
    The man who had to swing.

And strange it was to see him pass
    With a step so light and gay,
And strange it was to see him look
    So wistfully at the day,
And strange it was to think that he
    Had such a debt to pay.

*

For oak and elm have pleasant leaves
   That in the spring-time shoot:
But grim to see is the gallows-tree,
   With its adder-bitten root,
And, green or dry, a man must die
   Before it bears its fruit!

The loftiest place is that seat of grace
   For which all worldlings try:
But who would stand in hempen band
   Upon a scaffold high,
And through a murderer's collar take
   His last look at the sky?

It is sweet to dance to violins
   When Love and Life are fair:
To dance to flutes, to dance to lutes
   Is delicate and rare:
But it is not sweet with nimble feet
   To dance upon the air!

So with curious eyes and sick surmise
   We watched him day by day,
And wondered if each one of us
   Would end the self-same way,
For none can tell to what red Hell
   His sightless soul may stray.

At last the dead man walked no more
   Amongst the Trial Men,
And I knew that he was standing up
   In the black dock's dreadful pen,
And that never would I see his face
   In God's sweet world again.

Like two doomed ships that pass in storm
   We had crossed each other's way:
But we made no sign, we said no word,
   We had no word to say;
For we did not meet in the holy night,
   But in the shameful day.

A prison wall was round us both,
    Two outcast men we were:
The world had thrust us from its heart,
    And God from out His care:
And the iron gin that waits for Sin
    Had caught us in its snare.

III

In Debtors' Yard the stones are hard,
    And the dripping wall is high,
So it was there he took the air
    Beneath the leaden sky,
And by each side a Warder walked,
    For fear the man might die.

Or else he sat with those who watched
    His anguish night and day;
Who watched him when he rose to weep,
    And when he crouched to pray;
Who watched him lest himself should rob
    Their scaffold of its prey.

The Governor was strong upon
    The Regulations Act:
The Doctor said that Death was but
    A scientific fact:
And twice a day the Chaplain called,
    And left a little tract.

And twice a day he smoked his pipe,
    And drank his quart of beer:
His soul was resolute, and held
    No hiding-place for fear;
He often said that he was glad
    The hangman's hands were near.

But why he said so strange a thing
    No Warder dared to ask:
For he to whom a watcher's doom
    Is given as his task,
Must set a lock upon his lips,
    And make his face a mask.

Or else he might be moved, and try
   To comfort or console:
And what should Human Pity do
   Pent up in Murderers' Hole?
What word of grace in such a place
   Could help a brother's soul?

*

With slouch and swing around the ring
   We trod the Fools' Parade!
We did not care: we knew we were
   The Devil's Own Brigade:
And shaven head and feet of lead
   Make a merry masquerade.

We tore the tarry rope to shreds
   With blunt and bleeding nails;
We rubbed the doors, and scrubbed the floors,
   And cleaned the shining rails:
And, rank by rank, we soaped the plank,
   And clattered with the pails.

We sewed the sacks, we broke the stones,
   We turned the dusty drill:
We banged the tins, and bawled the hymns,
   And sweated on the mill:
But in the heart of every man
   Terror was lying still.

So still it lay that every day
   Crawled like a weed-clogged wave:
And we forgot the bitter lot
   That waits for fool and knave,
Till once, as we tramped in from work,
   We passed an open grave.

With yawning mouth the yellow hole
   Gaped for a living thing;
The very mud cried out for blood
   To the thirsty asphalte ring:
And we knew that ere one dawn grew fair
   Some prisoner had to swing.

Right in we went, with soul intent
    On Death and Dread and Doom:
The hangman, with his little bag,
    Went shuffling through the gloom:
And each man trembled as he crept
    Into his numbered tomb.

*

That night the empty corridors
    Were full of forms of Fear,
And up and down the iron town
    Stole feet we could not hear,
And through the bars that hide the stars
    White faces seemed to peer.

He lay as one who lies and dreams
    In a pleasant meadow-land,
The watchers watched him as he slept,
    And could not understand
How one could sleep so sweet a sleep
    With a hangman close at hand.

But there is no sleep when men must weep
    Who never yet have wept:
So we – the fool, the fraud, the knave –
    That endless vigil kept,
And through each brain on hands of pain
    Another's terror crept.

Alas! it is a fearful thing
    To feel another's guilt!
For, right within, the sword of Sin
    Pierced to its poisoned hilt,
And as molten lead were the tears we shed
    For the blood we had not spilt.

The Warders with their shoes of felt
    Crept by each padlocked door,
And peeped and saw, with eyes of awe,
    Grey figures on the floor,
And wondered why men knelt to pray
    Who never prayed before.

All through the night we knelt and prayed,
    Mad mourners of a corse!
The troubled plumes of midnight were
    The plumes upon a hearse:
And bitter wine upon a sponge
    Was the savour of Remorse.

*

The grey cock crew, the red cock crew,
    But never came the day:
And crooked shapes of Terror crouched,
    In the corners where we lay:
And each evil sprite that walks by night
    Before us seemed to play.

They glided past, they glided fast,
    Like travellers through a mist:
They mocked the moon in a rigadoon
    Of delicate turn and twist,
And with formal pace and loathsome grace
    The phantoms kept their tryst.

With mop and mow, we saw them go,
    Slim shadows hand in hand:
About, about, in ghostly rout
    They trod a saraband:
And the damned grotesques made arabesques,
    Like the wind upon the sand!

With the pirouettes of marionettes,
    They tripped on pointed tread:
But with flutes of Fear they filled the ear,
    As their grisly masque they led,
And loud they sang, and long they sang,
    For they sang to wake the dead.

'*Oho!*' they cried, '*The world is wide,*
    But fettered limbs go lame!
And once, or twice, to throw the dice
    Is a gentlemanly game,
But he does not win who plays with Sin
    In the secret House of Shame.'

No things of air these antics were,
    That frolicked with such glee:
To men whose lives were held in gyves,
    And whose feet might not go free,
Ah! wounds of Christ! they were living things,
    Most terrible to see.

Around, around, they waltzed and wound;
    Some wheeled in smirking pairs;
With the mincing step of a demirep
    Some sidled up the stairs:
And with subtle sneer, and fawning leer,
    Each helped us at our prayers.

The morning wind began to moan,
    But still the night went on:
Through its giant loom the web of gloom
    Crept till each thread was spun:
And, as we prayed, we grew afraid
    Of the Justice of the Sun.

The moaning wind went wandering round
    The weeping prison-wall:
Till like a wheel of turning steel
    We felt the minutes crawl:
O moaning wind! what had we done
    To have such a seneschal?

At last I saw the shadowed bars,
    Like a lattice wrought in lead,
Move right across the whitewashed wall
    That faced my three-plank bed,
And I knew that somewhere in the world
    God's dreadful dawn was red.

At six o'clock we cleaned our cells,
    At seven all was still,
But the sough and swing of a mighty wing
    The prison seemed to fill,
For the Lord of Death with icy breath
    Had entered in to kill.

He did not pass in purple pomp,
　Nor ride a moon-white steed.
Three yards of cord and a sliding board
　Are all the gallows' need:
So with rope of shame the Herald came
　To do the secret deed.

We were as men who through a fen
　Of filthy darkness grope:
We did not dare to breathe a prayer,
　Or to give our anguish scope:
Something was dead in each of us,
　And what was dead was Hope.

For Man's grim Justice goes its way
　And will not swerve aside:
It slays the weak, it slays the strong,
　It has a deadly stride:
With iron heel it slays the strong,
　The monstrous parricide!

We waited for the stroke of eight:
　Each tongue was thick with thirst:
For the stroke of eight is the stroke of Fate
　That makes a man accursed,
And Fate will use a running noose
　For the best man and the worst.

We had no other thing to do,
　Save to wait for the sign to come:
So, like things of stone in a valley lone,
　Quiet we sat and dumb:
But each man's heart beat thick and quick,
　Like a madman on a drum!

With sudden shock the prison-clock
　Smote on the shivering air,
And from all the gaol rose up a wail
　Of impotent despair,
Like the sound that frightened marshes hear
　From some leper in his lair.

And as one sees most dreadful things
   In the crystal of a dream,
We saw the greasy hempen rope
   Hooked to the blackened beam,
And heard the prayer the hangman's snare
   Strangled into a scream.

And all the woe that moved him so
   That he gave that bitter cry,
And the wild regrets, and the bloody sweats
   None knew so well as I:
For he who lives more lives than one
   More deaths than one must die.

IV

There is no chapel on the day
   On which they hang a man:
The Chaplain's heart is far too sick,
   Or his face is far too wan,
Or there is that written in his eyes
   Which none should look upon.

So they kept us close till nigh on noon,
   And then they rang the bell,
And the Warders with their jingling keys
   Opened each listening cell,
And down the iron stair we tramped,
   Each from his separate Hell.

Out into God's sweet air we went,
   But not in wonted way,
For this man's face was white with fear,
   And that man's face was grey,
And I never saw sad men who looked
   So wistfully at the day.

I never saw sad men who looked
   With such a wistful eye
Upon that little tent of blue
   We prisoners called the sky,
And at every careless cloud that passed
   In happy freedom by.

But there were those amongst us all
    Who walked with downcast head,
And knew that, had each got his due,
    They should have died instead:
He had but killed a thing that lived,
    Whilst they had killed the dead.

For he who sins a second time
    Wakes a dead soul to pain,
And draws it from its spotted shroud,
    And makes it bleed again,
And makes it bleed great gouts of blood,
    And makes it bleed in vain!

*

Like ape or clown, in monstrous garb
    With crooked arrows starred,
Silently we went round and round
    The slippery asphalte yard;
Silently we went round and round,
    And no man spoke a word.

Silently we went round and round,
    And through each hollow mind
The Memory of dreadful things
    Rushed like a dreadful wind,
And Horror stalked before each man,
    And Terror crept behind.

*

The Warders strutted up and down,
    And kept their herd of brutes,
Their uniforms were spick and span,
    And they wore their Sunday suits,
But we knew the work they had been at,
    By the quicklime on their boots.

For where a grave had opened wide,
    There was no grave at all:
Only a stretch of mud and sand
    By the hideous prison-wall,
And a little heap of burning lime,
    That the man should have his pall.

For he has a pall, this wretched man,
　　Such as few men can claim:
Deep down below a prison-yard,
　　Naked for greater shame,
He lies, with fetters on each foot,
　　Wrapt in a sheet of flame!

And all the while the burning lime
　　Eats flesh and bone away,
It eats the brittle bone by night,
　　And the soft flesh by day,
It eats the flesh and bone by turns,
　　But it eats the heart alway.

*

For three long years they will not sow
　　Or root or seedling there
For three long years the unblessed spot
　　Will sterile be and bare,
And look upon the wondering sky
　　With unreproachful stare.

They think a murderer's heart would taint
　　Each simple seed they sow.
It is not true! God's kindly earth
　　Is kindlier than men know,
And the red rose would but blow more red,
　　The white rose whiter blow.

Out of his mouth a red, red rose!
　　Out of his heart a white!
For who can say by what strange way,
　　Christ brings His will to light,
Since the barren staff the pilgrim bore
　　Bloomed in the great Pope's sight?

But neither milk-white rose nor red
　　May bloom in prison air;
The shard, the pebble, and the flint,
　　Are what they give us there:
For flowers have been known to heal
　　A common man's despair.

So never will wine-red rose or white,
   Petal by petal, fall
On that stretch of mud and sand that lies
   By the hideous prison-wall,
To tell the men who tramp the yard
   That God's Son died for all.

*

Yet though the hideous prison-wall
   Still hems him round and round,
And a spirit may not walk by night
   That is with fetters bound,
And a spirit may but weep that lies
   In such unholy ground,

He is at peace – this wretched man –
   At peace, or will be soon:
There is no thing to make him mad,
   Nor does Terror walk at noon,
For the lampless Earth in which he lies
   Has neither Sun nor Moon.

They hanged him as a beast is hanged:
   They did not even toll
A requiem that might have brought
   Rest to his startled soul,
But hurriedly they took him out,
   And hid him in a hole.

They stripped him of his canvas clothes,
   And gave him to the flies:
They mocked the swollen purple throat,
   And the stark and staring eyes:
And with laughter loud they heaped the shroud
   In which their convict lies.

The Chaplain would not kneel to pray
   By his dishonoured grave:
Nor mark it with that blessed Cross
   That Christ for sinners gave,
Because the man was one of those
   Whom Christ came down to save.

Yet all is well; he has but passed
   To life's appointed bourne:
And alien tears will fill for him
   Pity's long-broken urn,
For his mourners will be outcast men,
   And outcasts always mourn.

V

I know not whether Laws be right,
   Or whether Laws be wrong;
All that we know who lie in gaol
   Is that the wall is strong;
And that each day is like a year,
   A year whose days are long.

But this I know, that every Law
   That men have made for Man,
Since first Man took his brother's life,
   And the sad world began,
But straws the wheat and saves the chaff
   With a most evil fan.

This too I know – and wise it were
   If each could know the same –
That every prison that men build
   Is built with bricks of shame,
And bound with bars lest Christ should see
   How men their brothers maim.

With bars they blur the gracious moon,
   And blind the goodly sun:
And they do well to hide their Hell,
   For in it things are done
That Son of God nor son of Man
   Ever should look upon!

*

The vilest deeds like poison weeds,
   Bloom well in prison-air;
It is only what is good in Man
   That wastes and withers there:
Pale Anguish keeps the heavy gate,
   And the Warder is Despair.

For they starve the little frightened child
   Till it weeps both night and day:
And they scourge the weak, and flog the fool,
   And gibe the old and grey,
And some grow mad, and all grow bad,
   And none a word may say.

Each narrow cell in which we dwell
   Is a foul and dark latrine,
And the fetid breath of living Death
   Chokes up each grated screen,
And all, but Lust, is turned to dust
   In Humanity's machine.

The brackish water that we drink
   Creeps with a loathsome slime,
And the bitter bread they weigh in scales
   Is full of chalk and lime,
And Sleep will not lie down, but walks
   Wild-eyed, and cries to Time.

*

But though lean Hunger and green Thirst
   Like asp with adder fight,
We have little care of prison fare,
   For what chills and kills outright
Is that every stone one lifts by day
   Becomes one's heart by night.

With midnight always in one's heart,
   And twilight in one's cell,
We turn the crank, or tear the rope,
   Each in his separate Hell,
And the silence is more awful far
   Than the sound of a brazen bell.

And never a human voice comes near
   To speak a gentle word:
And the eye that watches through the door
   Is pitiless and hard:
And by all forgot, we rot and rot,
   With soul and body marred.

And thus we rust Life's iron chain
  Degraded and alone:
And some men curse, and some men weep,
  And some men make no moan:
But God's eternal Laws are kind
  And break the heart of stone.

*

And every human heart that breaks,
  In prison-cell or yard,
Is as that broken box that gave
  Its treasure to the Lord,
And filled the unclean leper's house
  With the scent of costliest nard.

Ah! happy they whose hearts can break
  And peace of pardon win!
How else may man make straight his plan
  And cleanse his soul from Sin?
How else but through a broken heart
  May Lord Christ enter in?

*

And he of the swollen purple throat,
  And the stark and staring eyes,
Waits for the holy hands that took
  The Thief to Paradise;
And a broken and a contrite heart
  The Lord will not despise.

The man in red who reads the Law
  Gave him three weeks of life,
Three little weeks in which to heal
  His soul of his soul's strife,
And cleanse from every blot of blood
  The hand that held the knife.

And with tears of blood he cleansed the hand,
  The hand that held the steel:
For only blood can wipe out blood,
  And only tears can heal:
And the crimson stain that was of Cain
  Became Christ's snow-white seal.

VI

In Reading gaol by Reading town
  There is a pit of shame,
And in it lies a wretched man
  Eaten by teeth of flame,
In a burning winding-sheet he lies,
  And his grave has got no name.

And there, till Christ call forth the dead,
  In silence let him lie:
No need to waste the foolish tear,
  Or heave the windy sigh:
The man had killed the thing he loved,
  And so he had to die.

And all men kill the thing they love,
  By all let this be heard,
Some do it with a bitter look,
  Some with a flattering word,
The coward does it with a kiss,
  The brave man with a sword!

RAVENNA

Newdigate Prize Poem
Recited in the Sheldonian Theatre,
Oxford June 26th, 1878
To my friend George Fleming,
author of The Nile Novel *and* Mirage

Ravenna

A year ago I breathed the Italian air, –
And yet, methinks this northern Spring is fair, –
These fields made golden with the flower of March,
The throstle singing on the feathered larch,
The cawing rooks, the wood-doves fluttering by,
The little clouds that race across the sky;
And fair the violet's gentle drooping head,
The primrose, pale for love uncomforted,
The rose that burgeons on the climbing briar,
The crocus-bed, (that seems a moon of fire
Round-girdled with a purple marriage-ring);
And all the flowers of our English Spring,
Fond snowdrops, and the bright-starred daffodil
Up starts the lark beside the murmuring mill,
And breaks the gossamer-threads of early dew;
And down the river, like a flame of blue,
Keen as an arrow flies the water-king,
While the brown linnets in the greenwood sing.
A year ago! – it seems a little time
Since last I saw that lordly southern clime,
Where flower and fruit to purple radiance blow,
And like bright lamps the fabled apples glow.
Full Spring it was – and by rich flowering vines,
Dark olive-groves and noble forest-pines,
I rode at will; the moist glad air was sweet,
The white road rang beneath my horse's feet,
And musing on Ravenna's ancient name,

I watched the day till, marked with wounds of flame,
The turquoise sky to burnished gold was turned.

O how my heart with boyish passion burned,
When far away across the sedge and mere
I saw that Holy City rising clear,
Crowned with her crown of towers! – On and on
I galloped, racing with the setting sun,
And ere the crimson after-glow was passed,
I stood within Ravenna's walls at last!

II

How strangely still! no sound of life or joy
Startles the air; no laughing shepherd-boy
Pipes on his reed, nor ever through the day
Comes the glad sound of children at their play:
O sad, and sweet, and silent! surely here
A man might dwell apart from troublous fear,
Watching the tide of seasons as they flow
From amorous Spring to Winter's rain and snow,
And have no thought of sorrow; – here, indeed,
Are Lethe's waters, and that fatal weed
Which makes a man forget his fatherland.

Ay! amid lotus-meadows dost thou stand,
Like Proserpine, with poppy-laden head,
Guarding the holy ashes of the dead.
For though thy brood of warrior sons hath ceased,
Thy noble dead are with thee! – they at least
Are faithful to thine honour: – guard them well,
O childless city! for a mighty spell,
To wake men's hearts to dreams of things sublime,
Are the lone tombs where rest the Great of Time.

III

Yon lonely pillar, rising on the plain,
Marks where the bravest knight of France was slain, –
The Prince of chivalry, the Lord of war,

Gaston de Foix: for some untimely Star
Led him against thy city, and he fell,
As falls some forest-lion fighting well.
Taken from life while life and love were new,
He lies beneath God's seamless veil of blue;
Tall lance-like reeds wave sadly o'er his head,
And oleanders bloom to deeper red,
Where his bright youth flowed crimson on the ground.

Look farther north unto that broken mound, –
There, prisoned now within a lordly tomb
Raised by a daughter's hand, in lonely gloom,
Huge-limbed Theodoric, the Gothic king,
Sleeps after all his weary conquering.
Time hath not spared his ruin, – wind and rain
Have broken down his stronghold; and again
We see that Death is mighty lord of all,
And king and clown to ashen dust must fall.

Mighty indeed *their* glory! yet to me
Barbaric king, or knight of chivalry,
Or the great queen herself, were poor and vain,
Beside the grave where Dante rests from pain.
His gilded shrine lies open to the air;
And cunning sculptor's hands have carven there
The calm white brow, as calm as earliest morn,
The eyes that flashed with passionate love and scorn,
The lips that sang of Heaven and of Hell,
The almond-face which Giotto drew so well,
The weary face of Dante; – to this day,
Here in his place of resting, far away
From Arno's yellow waters, rushing down
Through the wide bridges of that fairy town,
Where the tall tower of Giotto seems to rise
A marble lily under sapphire skies!
Alas! my Dante! thou hast known the pain
Of meaner lives, – the exile's galling chain,
How steep the stairs within kings' houses are,
And all the petty miseries which mar
Man's nobler nature with the sense of wrong.

Yet this dull world is grateful for thy song;
Our nations do thee homage, – even she,
That cruel queen of vine-clad Tuscany,
Who bound with crown of thorns thy living brow,
Hath decked thine empty tomb with laurels now,
And begs in vain the ashes of her son.

O mightiest exile! all thy grief is done:
Thy soul walks now beside thy Beatrice;
Ravenna guards thine ashes: sleep in peace.

IV
How lone this palace is; how grey the walls!
No minstrel now wakes echoes in these halls.
The broken chain lies rusting on the door,
And noisome weeds have split the marble floor:
Here lurks the snake, and here the lizards run
By the stone lions blinking in the sun.
Byron dwelt here in love and revelry
For two long years – a second Anthony,
Who of the world another Actium made!
Yet suffered not his royal soul to fade,
Or lyre to break, or lance to grow less keen,
'Neath any wiles of an Egyptian queen
For from the East there came a mighty cry,
And Greece stood up to fight for Liberty,
And called him from Ravenna: never knight
Rode forth more nobly to wild scenes of fight!
None fell more bravely on ensanguined field,
Borne like a Spartan back upon his shield!
O Hellas! Hellas! in thine hour of pride,
Thy day of might, remember him who died
To wrest from off thy limbs the trammelling chain:
O Salamis! O lone Plataean plain!
O tossing waves of wild Euboean sea!
O wind-swept heights of lone Thermopylae!
He loved you well – ay, not alone in word,
Who freely gave to thee his lyre and sword,
Like Aeschylos at well-fought Marathon:

And England, too, shall glory in her son,
Her warrior-poet, first in song and fight.
No longer now shall Slander's venomed spite
Crawl like a snake across his perfect name,
Or mar the lordly scutcheon of his fame.

For as the olive-garland of the race,
Which lights with joy each eager runner's face,
As the red cross which saveth men in war,
As a flame-bearded beacon seen from far
By mariners upon a storm-tossed sea, –
Such was his love for Greece and Liberty!

Byron, thy crowns are ever fresh and green:
Red leaves of rose from Sapphic Mitylene
Shall bind thy brows; the myrtle blooms for thee,
In hidden glades by lonely Castaly;
The laurels wait thy coming: all are thine,
And round thy head one perfect wreath will twine.

v

The pine-tops rocked before the evening breeze
With the hoarse murmur of the wintry seas,
And the tall stems were streaked with amber bright; –
I wandered through the wood in wild delight,
Some startled bird, with fluttering wings and fleet,
Made snow of all the blossoms; at my feet,
Like silver crowns, the pale narcissi lay,
And small birds sang on every twining spray.
O waving trees, O forest liberty!
Within your haunts at least a man is free,
And half forgets the wary world of strife:
The blood flows hotter, and a sense of life
Wakes i' the quickening veins, while once again
The woods are filled with gods we fancied slain.
Long time I watched, and surely hoped to see
Some goat-foot Pan make merry minstrelsy
Amid the reeds! some startled Dryad-maid
In girlish flight! or lurking in the glade,

The soft brown limbs, the wanton treacherous face
Of woodland god! Queen Dian in the chase,
White-limbed and terrible, with look of pride,
And leash of boar-hounds leaping at her side!
Or Hylas mirrored in the perfect stream.

O idle heart! O fond Hellenic dream!
Ere long, with melancholy rise and swell,
The evening chimes, the convent's vesper bell,
Struck on mine ears amid the amorous flowers.
Alas! alas! these sweet and honied hours
Had whelmed my heart like some encroaching sea,
And drowned all thoughts of black Gethsemane.

VI

O lone Ravenna! many a tale is told
Of thy great glories in the days of old:
Two thousand years have passed since thou didst see
Caesar ride forth to royal victory.
Mighty thy name when Rome's lean eagles flew
From Britain's isles to far Euphrates blue;
And of the peoples thou wast noble queen,
Till in thy streets the Goth and Hun were seen.
Discrowned by man, deserted by the sea,
Thou sleepest, rocked in lonely misery!
No longer now upon thy swelling tide,
Pine-forest-like, thy myriad galleys ride!
For where the brass-beaked ships were wont to float,
The weary shepherd pipes his mournful note;
And the white sheep are free to come and go
Where Adria's purple waters used to flow.

O fair! O sad! O Queen uncomforted!
In ruined loveliness thou liest dead,
Alone of all thy sisters; for at last
Italia's royal warrior hath passed
Rome's lordliest entrance, and hath worn his crown
In the high temples of the Eternal Town!
The Palatine hath welcomed back her king,
And with his name the seven mountains ring!

And Naples hath outlived her dream of pain,
And mocks her tyrant! Venice lives again,
New risen from the waters! and the cry
Of Light and Truth, of Love and Liberty,
Is heard in lordly Genoa, and where
The marble spires of Milan wound the air,
Rings from the Alps to the Sicilian shore,
And Dante's dream is now a dream no more.

But thou, Ravenna, better loved than all,
Thy ruined palaces are but a pall
That hides thy fallen greatness! and thy name
Burns like a grey and flickering candle-flame
Beneath the noonday splendour of the sun
Of new Italia! for the night is done,
The night of dark oppression, and the day
Hath dawned in passionate splendour: far away
The Austrian hounds are hunted from the land,
Beyond those ice-crowned citadels which stand
Girdling the plain of royal Lombardy,
From the far West unto the Eastern sea.

I know, indeed, that sons of thine have died
In Lissa's waters, by the mountain-side
Of Aspromonte, on Novara's plain, –
Nor have thy children died for thee in vain:
And yet, methinks, thou hast not drunk this wine
From grapes new-crushed of Liberty divine,
Thou hast not followed that immortal Star
Which leads the people forth to deeds of war.
Weary of life, thou liest in silent sleep,
As one who marks the lengthening shadows creep,
Careless of all the hurrying hours that run,
Mourning some day of glory, for the sun
Of Freedom hath not shewn to thee his face,
And thou hast caught no flambeau in the race.

Yet wake not from thy slumbers, – rest thee well,
Amidst thy fields of amber asphodel,
Thy lily-sprinkled meadows, – rest thee there,

To mock all human greatness: who would dare
To vent the paltry sorrows of his life
Before thy ruins, or to praise the strife
Of kings' ambition, and the barren pride
Of warring nations! wert not thou the Bride
Of the wild Lord of Adria's stormy sea!
The Queen of double Empires! and to thee
Were not the nations given as thy prey!
And now – thy gates lie open night and day,
The grass grows green on every tower and hall,
The ghastly fig hath cleft thy bastioned wall;
And where thy mailèd warriors stood at rest
The midnight owl hath made her secret nest.
O fallen! fallen! from thy high estate,
O city trammelled in the toils of Fate,
Doth nought remain of all thy glorious days,
But a dull shield, a crown of withered bays!

Yet who beneath this night of wars and fears,
From tranquil tower can watch the coming years;
Who can foretell what joys the day shall bring,
Or why before the dawn the linnets sing?
Thou, even thou, mayst wake, as wakes the rose
To crimson splendour from its grave of snows;
As the rich corn-fields rise to red and gold
From these brown lands, now stiff with Winter's cold;
As from the storm-rack comes a perfect star!

O much-loved city! I have wandered far
From the wave-circled islands of my home;
Have seen the gloomy mystery of the Dome
Rise slowly from the drear Campagna's way,
Clothed in the royal purple of the day:
I from the city of the violet crown
Have watched the sun by Corinth's hill go down
And marked the 'myriad laughter' of the sea
From starlit hills of flower-starred Arcady;
Yet back to thee returns my perfect love,
As to its forest-nest the evening dove.

O poet's city! one who scarce has seen
Some twenty summers cast their doublets green
For Autumn's livery, would seek in vain
To wake his lyre to sing a louder strain,
Or tell thy days of glory; – poor indeed
Is the low murmur of the shepherd's reed,
Where the loud clarion's blast should shake the sky,
And flame across the heavens! and to try
Such lofty themes were folly: yet I know
That never felt my heart a nobler glow
Than when I woke the silence of thy street
With clamorous trampling of my horse's feet,
And saw the city which now I try to sing,
After long days of weary travelling.

VII

Adieu, Ravenna! but a year ago,
I stood and watched the crimson sunset glow
From the lone chapel on thy marshy plain:
The sky was as a shield that caught the stain
Of blood and battle from the dying sun,
And in the west the circling clouds had spun
A royal robe, which some great God might wear,
While into ocean-seas of purple air
Sank the gold galley of the Lord of Light.

Yet here the gentle stillness of the night
Brings back the swelling tide of memory,
And wakes again my passionate love for thee:
Now is the Spring of Love, yet soon will come
On meadow and tree the Summer's lordly bloom;
And soon the grass with brighter flowers will blow,
And send up lilies for some boy to mow.
Then before long the Summer's conqueror,
Rich Autumn-time, the season's usurer,
Will lend his hoarded gold to all the trees,
And see it scattered by the spendthrift breeze;
And after that the Winter cold and drear.
So runs the perfect cycle of the year.

And so from youth to manhood do we go,
And fall to weary days and locks of snow.
Love only knows no winter; never dies:
Nor cares for frowning storms or leaden skies
And mine for thee shall never pass away,
Though my weak lips may falter in my lay.

Adieu ! Adieu ! yon silent evening star,
The night's ambassador, doth gleam afar,
And bid the shepherd bring his flocks to fold.
Perchance before our inland seas of gold
Are garnered by the reapers into sheaves,
Perchance before I see the Autumn leaves,
I may behold thy city; and lay down
Low at thy feet the poet's laurel crown.

Adieu ! Adieu ! yon silver lamp, the moon,
Which turns our midnight into perfect noon,
Doth surely light thy towers, guarding well
Where Dante sleeps, where Byron loved to dwell.

RAVENNA, MARCH 1877
OXFORD, MARCH 1878

NOTES

POEMS (1881)

Hélas!
1 (p. 1) *Hélas* French for 'Alas'
2 (p. 1) *a little rod* from I Samuel 14:43

ELEUTHERIA
3 (p. 2) *Eleutheria* Ancient Greek for 'Freedom'

Ave Imperatrix
4 (p. 2) *Ave Imperatrix* Latin for 'Hail, Empress'

Louis Napoleon
5 (p. 7) *Louis Napoleon* only son of the deposed Napoleon III, educated at the Royal Military Academy at Woolwich. At the age of twenty-three he was killed in action on 1 June 1879, fighting in South Africa for the British Army in the Zulu War
6 (p. 7) *Eagle of Austerlitz* Napoleon I whose greatest victory was in 1805 at Austerlitz, Czechoslovakia, against Russian and Austrian forces

Sonnet On the Massacre of the Christians in Bulgaria
7 (p. 8) *Christians in Bulgaria* Bulgaria had been part of the Turkish Ottoman Empire since the fourteenth century. An uprising by Christian Bulgarians against their Muslim oppressors in March 1876 brought horrific reprisals which became known as 'Bulgarian atrocities' and destabilised the region, sparking the Russo–Turkish War of 1877–8.
8 (p. 8) *Crescent moon* symbol on the Turkish flag

Quantum Mutata
9 (p. 8) *Quantum Mutata* Latin for 'How Much Changed'

Libertatis Sacra Fames
10 (p. 9) *Libertatis Sacra Fames* Latin for 'The Sacred Hunger for Liberty'
11 (p. 9) *anarchy* gives the political context for this poem, which was the terrorist activity by Russian revolutionaries in 1880 against repression by Emperor Alexander II

Theoretikos

12 (p. 9) *Theoretikos*   Ancient Greek for 'The Thinker'

The Garden of Eros

13 (p. 12) *gloomy Lord*   Pluto, King of the Underworld

14 (p. 13) *the boy who loved thee best*   the Romantic poet John Keats

15 (p. 13) *him at least thy love hath taught to sing*   the Romantic poet Lord Byron

16 (p. 14) *the Galilaean*   Jesus Christ

17 (p. 14) *an earthly paradise*   reference to *The Earthly Paradise* (1868–70), a collection of epic tales from classical and northern mythology by the Pre-Raphaelite writer and artist William Morris

18 (p. 15) *noisy eight*   Oxford University student boat-racing on the river Thames; each boat has eight rowers

19 (p. 15) *Bagley*   a wood near Oxford

20 (p. 15) *Dante and the seraph Gabriel*   reference to Dante Gabriel Rossetti, the Pre-Raphaelite poet and painter

ROSA MYSTICA

21 (p. 18) *Rosa Mystica*   Latin for 'Mystic Rose'

Requiescat

22 (p. 18) *Requiescat*   Latin for 'May She Rest'

Sonnet on Approaching Italy

23 (p. 19) *a second Peter*   Pope Pius IX who, from 1871, considered himself imprisoned in the Vatican because he refused to accept the new political status of Italy as a united kingdom with its capital city Rome no longer under Vatican control

San Miniato

24 (p. 19) *San Miniato*   a Renaissance monastery in Florence which Wilde visited in June 1875

25 (p. 19) *Angel-Painter*   Fra Angelico

Ave Maria Gratia Plena

26 (p. 20) *Ave Maria Gratia Plena*   Latin for 'Hail Mary, Full of Grace', a poem inspired by Wilde's visit to the Vatican Gallery in 1877

Urbs Sacra Aeterna

27 (p. 23) *Urbs Sacra Aeterna*   Latin for 'The Sacred, Eternal City'

28 (p. 23) *the prisoned shepherd*   Pope Pius IX

Easter Day

29 (p. 24) *Three crowns of gold*   the papal tiara
30 (p. 24) *To one who wandered*   Jesus Christ

E Tenebris

31 (p. 25) *E Tenebris*   Latin for 'Out of Darkness'

Vita Nuova

32 (p. 25) *Vita Nuova*   Latin for 'New Life', the title of a work by Dante
33 (p. 25) *unvintageable sea*   *The Odyssey* 2: 370, 'the unfruitful or barren sea'
34 (p. 25) *my final cast*   Luke 5:5–6
35 (p. 25) *white limbs ascend*   the resurrection of Christ and the birth of Venus

Madonna Mia

36 (p. 26) *Madonna Mia*   Latin for 'My Lady'
37 (p. 26) *a lily-girl*   Lillie Langtry, society beauty and mistress of the Prince of Wales

The New Helen

38 (p. 27) *Thetis' child*   Achilles

The Burden of Itys

39 (p. 32) *Nuneham*   village near Oxford, like Cumnor and Sandford, also mentioned in this poem
40 (p. 34) *Maeonia's bard*   Homer
41 (p. 34) *horn of Atalanta*   invocation of the poet Algernon Charles Swinburne, who published the verse drama *Atalanta in Calydon* (1865)
42 (p. 34) *Cumnor hills . . . Bagley wood*   places around Oxford to remind readers of Matthew Arnold whose poem 'The Scholar-Gipsy' (1853) is set there
43 (p. 35) *that brotherhood*   the Pre-Raphaelite Brotherhood, founded in 1848 by Dante Gabriel Rossetti and others
44 (p. 35) *son of Leto*   Apollo
45 (p. 40) *Magdalen's tall tower*   Wilde's college in Oxford

Magdalen Walks

46 (p. 42) *Magdalen Walks*   walks around Magdalen College, Oxford

Athanasia

47 (p. 43) *Athanasia*   Ancient Greek for 'Immortality'

48 (p. 43) *House of Art*   British Museum, where archaeological discoveries in Egypt and Greece were brought in the late 1870s

Serenade

49 (p. 45) *My Tyrian galley*   the speaker is Paris, the Trojan prince, as he serenades Helen, wife of the Greek king Menelaus, to sail away with him to Troy

La Bella Donna Della Mia Mente

50 (p. 47) *La Bella Donna Della Mia Mente*   Italian for 'The Beautiful Lady of My Memory'

Chanson

51 (p. 48) *Chanson*   French for 'Song'

Charmides

52 (p. 56) *Pale Pallas*   the goddess Athena
53 (p. 57) *gaunt owl*   Athena's sacred bird

The Grave of Keats

54 (p. 71) *Sebastian*   young officer in the Praetorian Guard and a favourite of the Roman Emperor Diocletian, martyred in AD 300 when his Christian faith was discovered. Wilde had been impressed by Guido Reni's painting *San Sebastian* in Genoa

55 (p. 71) *tears like mine*   Wilde prostrated himself on Keats's grave at the Protestant Cemetery in Rome on his Easter visit of 1877

56 (p. 71) *Isabella*   Keats's poem 'Isabella or the Pot of Basil'

Theocritus

57 (p. 71) *Theocritus*   the name of an Ancient Greek poet who lived in the third century BC, the author of pastoral *Idylls*

Amor Intellectualis

58 (p. 76) *Amor Intellectualis*   Latin for 'Intellectual Love'
59 (p. 76) *Sordello*   eponymous hero of the 1840 play by Robert Browning about the poet contemporary with Dante
60 (p. 76) *Endymion*   title of a poem by Keats published in 1818
61 (p. 76) *Tamburlaine*   hero of two plays by the Renaissance playwright Christopher Marlowe
62 (p. 76) *the Florentine*   Dante, author of *The Divine Comedy*

Santa Decca

63 (p. 76) *Santa Decca*   mountain on the Greek island of Corfu, now called Mount Pantokrator

A Vision

64 (p. 77) *Beatrice*   redemptive muse of Dante's *Divine Comedy*

65 (p. 77) *Euripides*   stands apart from the other two Ancient Greek tragedians because he departed from the conventions they deployed by using contemporary language, giving prominence to the roles of slaves and women and dressing his mythic figures in costumes to symbolise their suffering

The Grave of Shelley

66 (p. 78) *yon pyramid*   monument to Caius Cestius, a Roman magistrate who died *c.*30 BC, visible from the Protestant Cemetery in Rome where Shelley is remembered and which Wilde visited in 1877

Fabien dei Franchi

67 (p. 80) *Fabien dei Franchi*   Henry Irving, the great nineteenth-century actor, played the parts of both Louis and Fabien dei Franchi in Dion Boucicault's play *The Corsican Brothers* at the Lyceum Theatre, London, from 18 September 1880 to 9 April 1881

Phèdre

68 (p. 80) *Phèdre*   On 2 June 1878 Sarah Bernhardt performed the title role of Racine's tragedy at the Gaiety Theatre, London, in a visiting production by the Parisian Comédie-Française.

69 (p. 80) *Mirandola*   Giovanni Pico della Mirandola, 1463–94, Italian neo-Platonist and occult theologian

Portia

70 (p. 81) *Ellen Terry*   performed the role of Portia in Henry Irving's production of Shakespeare's *The Merchant of Venice* at the Lyceum Theatre, London, seen by Wilde on 28 November 1879

Queen Henrietta Maria

71 (p. 81) *Queen Henrietta Maria*   was the role played by Ellen Terry in the Lyceum Theatre's revival of W. G. Wills's *Charles I* in June 1879

72 (p. 81) *lone tent*   the camp scene in Act III was considered the best scene in the play

Camma

73 (p. 82) *Camma*   priestess of the goddess Artemis and the role played by Ellen Terry in Tennyson's verse drama *The Cup* at the Lyceum Theatre, London, in January 1881

74 (p. 82) *serpent of old Nile*   Cleopatra in Shakespeare's *Anthony and Cleopatra*

Panthea

75 (p. 86) *One great grand life*   derived from the sentiments described by Wordsworth in 'Lines Composed A Few Miles Above Tintern Abbey' (1798)

76 (p. 88) *New splendour*   reference to Wordsworth's 'Ode: Intimations of Immortality From Recollections of Early Childhood' (1807)

At Verona

77 (p. 89) *exile-wearied feet*   the speaker is Dante. Exiled from Florence in 1302, he was taken in by Can Grande della Scala of the Scaligeri family, lord of the city-state of Verona. Wilde draws on Dante Gabriel Rossetti's poem 'Dante at Verona'.

Quia Multum Amavi

78 (p. 92) *Quia Multum Amavi*   Latin for 'Because I Have Loved Too Much'. Title draws on Swinburne's 'Quia Multum Amavit' in *Songs Before Sunrise* (1871).

Silentium Amoris

79 (p. 92) *Silentium Amoris*   Latin for 'The Silence of Love'

Taedium Vitae

80 (p. 95) *Taedium Vitae*   Latin for 'Weariness of Life', the title heralds a conventional *fin-de-siècle* pose, expressing hedonistic exhaustion and boredom.

Humanitad

81 (p. 96) *Humanitad*   recalls the title 'Libertad' by Walt Whitman in *Leaves of Grass* (1855). The poem comments on the contemporary state of human nature, represented as declining from its former nobility. These sentiments are indebted to Swinburne's 'The Hymn of Man' in *Songs Before Sunrise* (1871).

82 (p. 99) *To burn with one clear flame*   The art-for-art's-sake creed voiced by Walter Pater in the 'Conclusion' to *Renaissance* centres on the injunction that consciousness should 'burn with a gem-like flame'.

83 (p. 99) *The gentle XAIPE*   an Ancient Greek greeting meaning both 'hail' and 'farewell'

84 (p. 100) *troubled waters*   recalls the setting of Matthew Arnold's poem 'Dover Beach'

85 (p. 100) *the sign Gorgonian*   monstrous

86 (p. 100) *By One who gave to thee his sword and lyre*   Lord Byron

87 (p. 101) *The grave Athenian*   Plato

88 (p. 101) *Polymnia*   muse of the mimic arts

89 (p. 101) *till he saw Thermopylae*   reference to the attack on Sparta by the Persian army under Xerxes

90 (p. 102) *Helvellyn*   one of Wordsworth's favourite mountains

91 (p. 102) *Rydalian laurels*   Wordsworth lived at Rydal Mount, Ambleside

92 (p. 102) *Ichabod*   biblical personage whose name means 'the glory is departed', epitomising the crux of this poem. See I Samuel 4:21–2.

93 (p. 102) *that last dear son of Italy*   Giuseppe Mazzini (1805–72), Italian revolutionary and nationalist who proclaimed the Roman Republic in 1849

94 (p. 102) *Giotto's tower*   Giotto designed the campanile or bell tower of Santa Maria del Fiore, the Cathedral in Florence.

95 (p. 103) *the Nine*   the nine muses

96 (p. 104) *At Munich on the marble architrave*   the architrave of the Temple of Aegina, housed in the Glyptothek in Munich

97 (p. 104) *Aspromonte*   the Battle of Aspromonte, 29 August 1862, in which Garibaldi was decisively defeated by the forces of King Victor Emmanuel

98 (p. 106) *the Body and the Spirit one*   recalls the redemptive vision of Wordsworth's 'Tintern Abbey'

Flower of Love

99 (p. 109) ῗμωλ῏πιλςοχ Ὑ⊓ςῶχ   bittersweet love, a citation from Sappho's fragment 81

UNCOLLECTED POEMS
°ῗμιξοξ, αἰμιξοξ εἰπῨ, τὸ δΥ εὖ ξιλ.φ

100 (p. 112) °ῗμιξοξ . . . ξιλ.τ φ   citation from Aeschylus's *Agamemnon*, 1.121, 'Sing the song of woe, the song of woe, but may the good prevail'

101 (p. 112) *ladders to be nearer God*   recalls Jacob's ladder, Genesis 28: 12

The True Knowledge . . .

102 (p. 112) . . . ἀξαηλαέφχ δΥῨψει . νά   'like the grassy head/ In the morning, life is mown; and this man is,/ And that man is not' (Gilbert Murray's translation, *Euripides*, 1902, p. 326)

103 (p. 112) *Thou knowest all*   the speaker Wilde addresses the spirit of his father who died on 19 April 1876. This poem was first published in the *Irish Monthly*, September 1876

On the Sale by Auction of Keats's Love Letters
104 (p. 117) *Endymion*   the title of a poem Keats wrote in 1817, and in Greek mythology the name of the setting sun with which the moon is in love
105 (p. 117) *a far Eastern town*   Jerusalem

Fantasies Décoratives
106 (p. 118) *Le Panneau*   French for The Snare

With a Copy of 'A House of Pomegranates'
107 (p. 122) *A House of Pomegranates*   the title of Wilde's second collection of fairy tales, published in 1891 and dedicated to his wife

To L.L.
108 (p. 122) *L.L.*   Lillie Langtry (1853–1929)

GLOSSARY

Actaeon   a hunter who surprised Diana bathing and was punished by being changed into a stag and torn to pieces by his own hounds

Adonis   a beautiful boy, beloved by Venus, and killed by a boar while hunting

Amaryllis   a pastoral sweetheart

Antinous   the page of Hadrian the Roman Emperor, a model of manly beauty

Aphrodite   the Greek goddess of love. Her name means 'foam born', and she was said to be born from the foam of the sea. Her Latin name is Venus.

Arachne   a skilful needlewoman, changed by the jealous Minerva into a spider

Arcady   a pastoral paradise

Ariadne   daughter of King Minos. She fell in love with Theseus and helped him to escape from the Minotaur's labyrinth. They fled Crete together but she was abandoned by Theseus on the island of Naxos.

Artemis   Apollo's twin sister, known in Latin as Diana. Goddess of hunting and wildlife, she was chaste and easily roused to fatal jealousy.

Atalanta   a princess, abandoned by her father at birth. She was suckled by bears and became a fierce virgin huntress. She rejected all suitors and was finally changed into a lion by Rhea, the mother of the gods.

Athena   a virgin goddess who was born fully grown and armed from the head of Zeus her father. Worshipped at the Parthenon in Athens, she is the goddess of war and invention. Her Latin name is Minerva.

Bacchus   the Roman god of wine whose Greek name is Dionysus

Calypso   the queen of the island Ogygia where Odysseus was shipwrecked and stayed for seven years

Cephissos   a river in Greece

Cynthia   the moon, another name for Artemis or Diana who was represented by the moon

Cytheraea   a Phoenician trading-post where Aphrodite was worshipped. Homer uses Cytheraean as an epithet for Aphrodite.

Danae   daughter of King Acrisius. She was beloved by Zeus who visited her as a shower of gold and she gave birth to Zeus's son Perseus.

Daphne   a virginal nymph, transformed into a laurel tree by Gaea to help her escape from the arms of Apollo

Diana   Latin name for Artemis

Dionysus   son of Zeus. Crowned with vine leaves and bunches of grapes, he is the god of wine. His Latin name is Bacchus.

Dis   god of the underworld

Endymion   the setting sun, beloved by the moon, condemned to endless sleep and everlasting youth

Eros   the god of love. His Latin name is Cupid.

Euphorion   ill-fated son of Helen of Troy and Faust in Goethe's *Faust II*

Ganymede   the beautiful boy cup-bearer of Zeus

Hecate   mother of Medea and Circe, she presided over magic and taught witchcraft

Hector   eldest and most noble son of King Priam of Troy. He was killed by Achilles and his body was dragged three times around the walls of Troy.

Helena   or Helen, the beautiful daughter of Zeus and Leda, wife of the Spartan King Menelaus. Her elopement with Paris, prince of Troy, sparked off the ten years' Trojan War.

Herakles   or Hercules, son of Alcmene and Zeus, a Greek hero of fabulous strength

Hesperus   the evening star

Hylas   a boy beloved by Hercules, snatched away by nymphs while drawing water from a fountain

Ida   Mount Ida in Greece and the name of a nymph who nursed the baby Zeus

Isis   an Egyptian Delta goddess, sister and wife of Osiris. She reassembled his dismembered and scattered body, embalmed and preserved it, then conceived a son, Horus, from it.

Itys   son of Procne and King Tereus of Thrace. When Procne discovered that Tereus had raped her sister Philomel and cut out her tongue, she took revenge on him by killing Itys and serving him up to Tereus for dinner. A benevolent god turned Procne into a swallow, Philomel into a nightingale and Itys into a goldfinch.

Juno   Latin name for Hera, queen of Olympus and wife of Jupiter or Zeus

Jove   Latin name for Zeus, overlord of Olympus

Lethe   river of forgetfulness running through the underworld

Marsyas   a satyr who played the flute, punished for challenging Apollo to a musical competition by being skinned alive

Medea   a sorceress who married Jason and helped him to find the golden fleece

Memnon   legendary statue of the Nile, said to sing at dawn

Melpomene   the muse of tragedy

Mercury   Roman god of trade

Mnemosyne   Memory, the mother of the muses

Naiad   nymph of streams

Narcissus   beautiful boy who fell in love with his own reflection in the water

Niobe   personification of female sorrow

Olympus   the home of the gods

Oread   nymph of mountains and grottoes

Osiris   Egyptian god, brother and husband of Isis, murdered and dismembered by his evil brother Set

Pan   personification of the deity pervading all creation, a lustful half-goat, half-man.

Pandion   King of Athens, father of Procne and Philomel

Panthea   an Oceanid who represents the concept of faith. Her name derived from the term 'pantheism'.

Persephone   daughter of Demeter, carried off by Pluto to Hades and made his queen. Her bondage to him is symbolised by the pomegranate.

Perseus   son of the mortal Danae and Zeus, a hero who killed the monster Medusa

Philomel   raped and mutilated by her brother-in-law King Tereus, afterwards transformed into a nightingale by a benevolent deity

Polypheme   companion of Hercules on his voyage to Colchis. He brought Hercules the news that his beloved Hylas had been snatched away by nymphs.

Poseidon   god of the sea

Proserpina   Greek name for Persephone

Proteus   Poseidon's herdsman, a shape-changer and a prophet

Salmacis   a nymph who fell in love with Hermaphroditus. She wished for complete union with him and immediately their two bodies became as one, of which it was said 'in their double form they are neither man nor woman; they seem to have no sex yet to be of both sexes'.

Saturn   Roman agricultural god, personifies abundance

Sphinx   a mysterious female monster with the body of a lion and the head of a human

Syrinx   a nymph, sister of Daphne

Theseus   Athenian hero who killed the Minotaur and was the lover of Ariadne

Thoth   Egyptian moon-god, patron of science and literature, wisdom and inventions, represented with the head of an ibis

Titans   the generation of gods deposed by Zeus

Venus   Latin name for Aphrodite, goddess of love

INDEX OF POEM TITLES

INDEX OF FIRST LINES

The Wordsworth Poetry Library

Works of

Matthew Arnold

William Blake

The Brontë Sisters

Rupert Brooke

Robert Browning

Elizabeth Barrett Browning

Robert Burns

Lord Byron

Geoffrey Chaucer

G. K. Chesterton

John Clare

Samuel Taylor Coleridge

Emily Dickinson

John Donne

John Dryden

Thomas Hardy

George Herbert

Gerard Manley Hopkins

A. E. Housman

James Joyce

John Keats

Rudyard Kipling

D. H. Lawrence

Henry Wadsworth Longfellow

Macaulay

Andrew Marvell

John Milton

Wilfred Owen

'Banjo' Paterson

Edgar Allen Poe

Alexander Pope

John Wilmot, Earl of Rochester

Christina Rossetti

Sir Walter Scott

William Shakespeare

P. B. Shelley

Edmund Spenser

Algernon Swinburne

Alfred Lord Tennyson

Edward Thomas

Walt Whitman

Oscar Wilde

William Wordsworth

W. B. Yeats

Anthologies & Collections

Restoration and
Eighteenth-Century Verse

Nineteenth-Century Verse

First World War Poetry

The Metaphysical Poets

Golden Treasury of Verse

Love Poetry

Sonnets